JUSTIN MCJUZAN

indonesia malaysia & singapore

To Reuben, who married me before I learned to cook.

Completely revised and updated in 2011
First published in 1976

This edition published in 2013 by Hardie Grant Books

Hardie Grant Books (Australia)
Ground Floor, Building 1
658 Church Street
Richmond, Victoria 3121
www.hardiegrant.com.au

Hardie Grant Books (UK)
Dudley House, North Suite
34–35 Southampton Street
London WC2E 7HF
www.hardiegrant.co.uk

A Cataloguing-in-Publication entry is available from the catalogue of the National Library of
Australia at www.nla.gov.au
The Complete Asian Cookbook: Indonesia, Malaysia & Singapore
ISBN 978 1 74270 684 9

Publishing Director: Paul McNally
Project Editor: Rihana Ries
Editor: Ariana Klepac
Design Manager: Heather Menzies
Design Concept: Murray Batten
Typesetting: Megan Ellis
Photographer: Alan Benson
Stylist: Vanessa Austin
Production: Todd Rechner

Colour reproduction by Splitting Image Colour Studio
Printed and bound in China by 1010 Printing International Limited

Find this book on **Cooked.**

THE
Complete
Asian
COOKBOOK

indonesia
malaysia &
singapore

CHARMAINE SOLOMON

hardie grant books
MELBOURNE · LONDON

Contents

Foreword   6

INDONESIA
Introduction   14
Your Indonesian shelf   17
1. Rice and Noodles   18
2. Soups and Snacks   24
3. Fish and Seafood   35
4. Poultry and Eggs   52
5. Meat   65
6. Vegetables   85
7. Accompaniments   100
8. Sweets and Desserts   113

MALAYSIA
Introduction   116
Your Malaysian shelf   118
1. Rice, Noodles and Soups   119
2. Fish and Seafood   126
3. Meat   136
4. Vegetables and Accompaniments   147
5. Sweets and Desserts   155

SINGAPORE

Introduction   159

Your Singaporean shelf   162

1. Rice, Noodles and Snacks   163

2. Fish and Seafood   175

3. Meat   184

4. Accompaniments   196

5. Sweets and Desserts   200

Glossary   **205**

Index   **212**

Contents ❖

Foreword

Just as France has its robust country fare as well as its subtle haute cuisine, so too does Asia have a range of culinary delights that can be simple, complex, fiery, mild, tantalising — and compulsive! Not all Asian food is exotic or wildly unusual. Noodle and rice dishes are as commonplace as the pastas and potatoes of the West. Many of the ingredients will be familiar to anyone who knows their way around a kitchen. The main differences have arisen just as they have arisen in other parts of the world — through the use of available ingredients. Thus there is a reliance on some herbs and spices less well known in the West. Meat is often replaced by the nutritious by-products of the soy bean and by protein-rich fish sauces and shrimp pastes.

True, some of the more unusual ingredients take a little getting used to. But once you have overcome what resistance you may have towards the idea of raw fish or dried shrimp paste or seaweed, you'll find that these (and other) ingredients are no less delicious than – and certainly as exciting as – those you use in your favourite dishes.

The introduction to each chapter will give you a good idea of what to expect in the way of out-of-the-ordinary ingredients. Almost without exception, those called for are readily available in most large supermarkets or Asian grocery stores; in the rare case they are not, suitable substitutes have been given.

Those of you already familiar with Southeast Asian cuisines will, I hope, find recipes to interest and excite you in these pages; and I think you will be tempted to explore dishes with which you are less well acquainted. For those of you who are coming to Southeast Asian cooking for the first time, I have taken care to make sure the essential steps are clear and precise, with detailed instructions on the following pages for cooking the much-used ingredients (such as rice, noodles, coconut milk and chilli), and pointers on how to joint a chicken, portion fish and select and season a wok.

For most countries, the names of the recipes have been given in the dominant or most common language or dialect of the country concerned, followed by the English name in italics.

In Malaysia and Indonesia, some years ago, a new unified system of spelling was introduced. The 'ch' in Malay and the 'tj' in Indonesian were replaced by the letter 'c' – thus *blachan* became *blacan* and *tjumi-tjumi* (squid) became *cumi-cumi*; the letters 'oe' in Indonesian became the letter 'u' thus *ulek* instead of *oelek*; and the letters 'dj' in Indonesian became the letter 'j' – thus *bajak* instead of *badjak*. Generally, the letter 'a' in Asian words is pronounced as the 'a' in father, never as in cat; the letter 'u' is rather like the 'oo' in look, never as in duty; and the letters 'th' are generally pronounced like an ordinary 't' (slightly aspirated), never as in breath or breathe.

Eating for health

Most Asian food is healthy. Many spices and ingredients such as turmeric, garlic and ginger have proven health-giving properties. However, with today's emphasis on weight control I have made modifications in the quantity and type of fat used for cooking. I have found it is possible to get very good results using almost half the amount of fat called for in many traditional dishes.

In certain Southeast Asian countries, lard is used as a cooking medium. In my kitchen I substitute a light vegetable oil. The flavour will be slightly different, but the way it sits on your stomach will be different too. Coconut oil, used frequently in Malaysia and other coconut-growing countries, is now, in its extra-virgin form, considered a healthy oil. If you are battling high cholesterol, when using coconut milk cut down on the quantity and substitute a similar amount of skim milk.

All of these recipes are adaptable to low-fat diets with very little sacrifice of flavour, since most of the exotic tastes come from herbs, spices and sauces.

Cooking with a wok

If I had to choose one cooking pan to be marooned on a desert island with, I'd choose a wok. It would cope with any kind of food that happened to be available. In it you can boil, braise, fry and steam, and while you can do all these things in pans you already possess, the wok is almost indispensable for the stir-frying technique that many Asian dishes call for. Because of its rounded shape and high, flaring sides you can toss with abandon and stir-fry ingredients without their leaping over the sides; and because the wok is made of thin iron you get the quick, high heat necessary to much Asian cooking.

Though a wok is best used with gas, it is possible to get good results with electricity. Because quick, high heat is required in stir-frying, turn the hotplate on to the highest heat and place the wok directly on it; it is possible to buy woks with a flat base for better contact, or invest in an electric wok where the heating element is built into the pan. The 30–35 cm (12–14 in) wok is most useful. You can cook small quantities in a large wok, but not vice versa.

The wok made of stainless steel is a modern innovation, but a modestly priced iron wok heats up quickly and evenly and, if you remember to dry it well after washing, it will not rust.

Before use, an iron wok must be seasoned. Prepare it by washing thoroughly in hot water and detergent. Some woks, when new, have a lacquer-like coating, which must be removed by almost filling the wok with water, adding about 2 tablespoons bicarbonate of soda (baking soda) and boiling for about 15 minutes. This softens the coating and it can be scrubbed off with a fine scourer. If some of the coating still remains, repeat the process until the wok is free from any lacquer on the inside. To season the new wok, dry it well, put over gentle heat and, when the metal heats up, wipe over the entire inner surface with some crumpled paper towel dipped in peanut oil. Repeat a number of times with more oil-soaked paper until the paper stays clean. Allow to cool. Your wok is now ready for use.

After cooking in it, do not scrub the wok with steel wool or abrasives of any kind. Soak in hot water to soften any remaining food, then rub gently with a sponge, using hot water and detergent – this preserves the surface. Make sure the wok is quite dry, because if moisture stays left in the pan it will rust. Heat the wok gently to ensure complete dryness, then rub over the inside surface with lightly oiled paper. A well-used wok will soon turn black, but this is normal – and the more a wok is used, the better it is to cook in.

Deep-frying

A wok is an efficient pan for deep-frying as it has a wider surface area than a regular frying pan. Be sure that the wok is sitting securely on the stove. Fill the wok no more than two-thirds full and heat the oil over medium heat.

To check the temperature for deep-frying, use a kitchen thermometer if you have one – on average, 180°C (350°F) is the correct temperature. To test without a thermometer, a cube of bread dropped into the oil will brown in 15 seconds at 180°C (350°F), and in 10 seconds if the temperature is 190°C (375°F).

The higher temperature may be suitable to use for foods that don't have great thickness, but if something needs to cook through, such as chicken pieces, use a lower temperature of around 160°C (320°F) – in this case a cube of bread will take nearly 30 seconds to brown. If the temperature is not hot enough, the food will absorb oil and become greasy. If you overheat the oil it could catch fire.

Use refined peanut oil, light olive oil, canola or rice bran oil and lower the food in gently with tongs or a slotted spoon so as not to splash yourself with hot oil. Removing the fried food to a colander lined with crumpled paper towel will help to remove any excess oil.

After cooling, oil may be poured through a fine metal skimmer and stored in an airtight jar away from the light. It may be used within a month or so, adding fresh oil to it when heating. After a couple of uses, it will need to be disposed of properly.

Coconut milk

I have heard many people refer to the clear liquid inside a coconut as 'coconut milk'. I have even read it in books. So, at the risk of boring those who already know, let's establish right away what coconut milk really is. It's the milky liquid extracted from the grated flesh of mature fresh coconuts or reconstituted from desiccated (shredded) coconut.

Coconut milk is an important ingredient in the cookery of nearly all Asian countries. It is used in soups, curries, savoury meat or seafood mixtures and all kinds of desserts. It has an unmistakable flavour and richness and should be used in recipes that call for it.

When the first edition of this book was published in 1975, the only good way to obtain coconut milk outside the countries where coconuts grow was to extract it yourself. These days coconut milk is widely available in tins from supermarkets. Problematically, the quality between brands varies enormously so it is worth comparing a few brands and checking the ingredients list – it should only have coconut and water in it. It should smell and taste fresh and clean and be neither watery nor solid. It is better to avoid brands that include stabilisers and preservatives. Shake the tin well before opening to disperse the richness evenly throughout. Brands in Tetra Paks tend not to be lumpy or watery.

Delicious as it is, coconut milk is full of saturated fat. With this in mind, I suggest that only when coconut cream is required should you use the tinned coconut milk undiluted. Where a recipe calls for thick coconut milk, dilute the tinned product with half its volume in water (for example, 250 ml/8½ fl oz/1 cup tinned coconut milk and 125 ml/4 fl oz/½ cup water). Where coconut milk is required, dilute the tinned coconut milk with an equal amount of water. Where thin coconut milk is required, dilute the tinned coconut milk with two parts by volume of water (for example, 250 ml/8½ fl oz/1 cup tinned coconut milk and 500 ml/17 fl oz/2 cups water).

If you would like to make your own coconut milk, the extraction method is included below. Traditionally, coconut milk is extracted in two stages – the first yield being the 'thick milk', the second extraction producing 'thin milk'. Use a mixture of first and second extracts when a recipe calls for coconut milk unless thick milk or thin milk is specified. Sometimes they are added at different stages of the recipe. Some recipes use 'coconut cream'. This is the rich layer that rises to the top of the thick milk (or first extract) after it has been left to stand for a while.

Making coconut milk from scratch

Using desiccated (shredded) coconut

Makes 375 ml (12½ fl oz/1½ cups) thick coconut milk
Makes 500 ml (17 fl oz/2 cups) thin coconut milk

Many cooks use desiccated coconut for making coconut milk. It is much easier and quicker to prepare than grating fresh coconut, and in curries you cannot tell the difference.

180 g (6½ oz/2 cups) desiccated (shredded) coconut

1.25 litres (42 fl oz/5 cups) hot water

Put the desiccated coconut into a large bowl and pour over 625 ml (21 fl oz/2½ cups) of the hot water then allow to cool to lukewarm. Knead firmly with your hands for a few minutes, then strain through a fine sieve or a piece of muslin (cheesecloth), pressing or squeezing out as much liquid as possible; this is the thick coconut milk.

Repeat the process using the same coconut and remaining hot water. This extract will yield the thin coconut milk. (Because of the moisture retained in the coconut the first time, the second extract usually yields more milk.)

Alternatively, to save time, you can use an electric blender or food processor. Put the desiccated coconut and 625 ml (21 fl oz/2½ cups) of the hot water into the blender and process for 30 seconds, then strain through a fine sieve or piece of muslin (cheesecloth), squeezing out all the moisture. Repeat, using the same coconut and remaining hot water.

Note: *Sometimes a richer milk is required. For this, hot milk replaces the water and only the first extract is used. However, a second extract will yield a flavoursome and reasonably rich grade of coconut milk that can be used in soups, curries or other dishes.*

Using fresh coconut

Makes 375 ml (12½ fl oz/1½ cups) thick coconut milk
Makes 500 ml (17 fl oz/2 cups) thin coconut milk

In Asian countries, fresh coconut is used and a coconut grater is standard equipment in every household. Grating fresh coconut is easy if you have the right implement for the job. However, if you are able to get fresh coconuts and do not have such an implement, use a food processor to pulverise the coconut and then extract the milk.

1 fresh coconut

1 litre (34 fl oz/4 cups) water or milk

Preheat the oven to 180°C (350°F). Crack the coconut in half by hitting it with the back of a heavy kitchen chopper. Once a crack has appeared, insert the thin edge of the blade and prise it open. Save the sweet liquid inside for drinking. If you do not own a coconut grater, put the two halves on a baking tray and bake in the oven for 15–20 minutes, or until the flesh starts to come away from the shell. Lift it out with the point of a knife, and peel away the thin dark brown skin that clings to the white portion. Cut into chunks.

Put the coconut flesh into a food processor with 500 ml (17 fl oz/2 cups) of the water and process until the coconut is completely pulverised. Strain the liquid using a sieve or muslin (cheesecloth) to extract the thick coconut milk. Repeat this process using the same coconut and remaining water to extract the thin milk. Left-over freshly extracted or bought coconut milk may be frozen – ice cube trays are ideal.

Chillies

Fresh chillies are used in most Asian food, particularly that of Southeast Asia. If mild flavouring is required, simply wash the chilli and add it to the dish when simmering, then lift out and discard the chilli before serving. But if you want the authentic fiery quality of the dish, you need to seed and chop the chillies first. To do this, remove the stalk of each chilli and cut in half lengthways to remove the central membrane and seeds – the seeds are the hottest part of the chilli. If you wish to make fiery hot sambals, the chillies are used seeds and all – generally ground or puréed in a food processor.

If you handle chillies without wearing gloves, wash your hands thoroughly with soap and warm water afterwards. Chillies can be so hot that even two or three good washings do not stop the tingling sensation, which can go on for hours. If this happens, remember to keep your hands well away from your eyes, lips or where the skin is especially sensitive. If you have more chillies than you need, they can be wrapped in plastic wrap and frozen, then added to dishes and used without thawing.

Dried chillies come in many shapes and sizes. Generally I use the large variety. If frying them as an accompaniment to a meal, use them whole, dropping them straight into hot oil. If they are being soaked and ground as part of the spicing for a sambal, sauce or curry, first cut off the stalk end and shake the chilli so that the seeds fall out. They are safe enough to handle until they have been soaked and ground, but if you handle them after this has been done, remember to wash your hands at once with soap and water.

Dried chillies, though they give plenty of heat and flavour, do not have the same volatile oils as fresh chillies and so do not have as much effect on the skin.

Rice varieties

One of the oldest grains in the world, and a staple food of more than half the world's population, rice is by far the most important item in the daily diet throughout Asia.

There are thousands of varieties. Agricultural scientists involved in producing new and higher yielding strains of rice will pick differences that are not apparent to even the most enthusiastic rice eater. But, from the Asian consumer's viewpoint, rice has qualities that a Westerner might not even notice – colour, fragrance, flavour, texture.

Rice buyers are so trained to recognise different types of rice that they can hold a few grains in the palm to warm it, sniff it through the hole made by thumb and forefinger, and know its age, variety, even perhaps where it was grown. Old rice is sought after and prized more than new rice because it tends to be fluffy and separate when cooked, even if the cook absent-mindedly adds too much water. Generally speaking, the white polished grains – whether long and fine or small and pearly (much smaller than what we know as short-grain rice) – are considered best.

In Malaysia, Indonesia and Singapore, rice is preferred dry and separate, but it is cooked without salt.

Rice is sold either packaged or in bulk. Polished white rice is available as long-, medium- or short-grain. Unpolished or natural rice is available as medium- or long-grain; and in many countries it is possible to buy an aromatic table rice grown in Bangladesh, called basmati rice. In dishes where spices and flavourings are added and cooked with the rice, any type of long-grain rice may be used. In each recipe the type of rice best suited is recommended, but as a general rule, remember that medium-grain or short-grain rice gives a clinging result and long-grain rice, properly cooked, is fluffy and separate.

Preparing rice

To wash or not to wash? Among Asian cooks there will never be agreement on whether rice should be washed or not. Some favour washing the rice several times, then leaving it to soak for a while. Other good cooks insist that washing rice is stupid and wasteful, taking away what vitamins and nutrients are left after the milling process.

I have found that most rice sold in Australia does not need washing but that rice imported in bulk and packaged here picks up a lot of dust and dirt and needs thorough washing and draining.

In a recipe, if rice is to be fried before any liquid is added, the washed rice must be allowed enough time to thoroughly drain and dry, between 30 and 60 minutes. Rice to be steamed must be soaked overnight. Rice for cooking by the absorption method may be washed (or not), drained briefly and added to the pan immediately.

Cooking rice

For a fail-safe way of cooking rice perfectly every time, put the required amount of rice and water into a large saucepan with a tight-fitting lid (see the measures below). Bring to the boil over high heat, cover, then reduce the heat to low and simmer for 20 minutes. Remove from the heat, uncover the pan and allow the steam to escape for a few minutes before fluffing up the rice with a fork.

Transfer the rice to a serving dish with a slotted metal spoon – don't use a wooden spoon or it will crush the grains. You will notice that long-grain rice absorbs considerably more water than short-grain rice, so the two kinds are not interchangeable in recipes. Though details are given in every rice recipe, here is a general rule regarding proportions of rice and liquid.

Noodles

Long-grain rice	Short- or medium-grain rice
200 g (7 oz/1 cup) rice use 500 ml (17 fl oz/2 cups) water	220 g (8 oz/1 cup) rice use 375 ml (12½ fl oz/1½ cups) water
400 g (14 oz/2 cups) rice use 875 ml (29½ fl oz/3½ cups) water	440 g (15½ oz/2 cups) rice use 625 ml (21 fl oz/2½ cups) water
600 g (1 lb 5 oz/3 cups) rice use 1.25 litres (42 fl oz/5 cups) water	660 g (1 lb 7 oz/3 cups) rice use 875 ml (29½ fl oz/3½ cups) water
Use 500 ml (17 fl oz/2 cups) water for the first cup of rice, then 375 ml (12½ fl oz/1½ cups) water for each additional cup of rice.	Use 375 ml (12½ fl oz/1½ cups) water for the first cup of rice, then 250 ml (8½ fl oz/1 cup) water for each additional cup of rice.

There are many different types of noodles available and different Asian countries have specific uses and preferences. Almost all of these varieties are available from large supermarkets or Asian grocery stores.

Dried egg noodles: Perhaps the most popular noodles, these are made of wheat flour. Dried egg noodles must be soaked in hot water for about 10 minutes before cooking. This is not mentioned in the cooking instructions, yet it does make cooking them so much easier – as the noodles soften the strands spread and separate and the noodles cook more evenly than when they are dropped straight into boiling water.

A spoonful of oil in the water prevents boiling over. When water returns to the boil, cook fine noodles for 2–3 minutes and thick noodles for 3–4 minutes. Do not overcook. Drain immediately, then run cold water through the noodles to rinse off any excess starch and cool them so they don't continue to cook in their own heat. Drain thoroughly. To reheat, pour boiling water over the noodles in a colander. Serve with stir-fried dishes or use in soups and braised noodle dishes.

Dried rice noodles: There are various kinds of flat rice noodles. Depending on the type of noodle and thickness of the strands, they have to be soaked in cold water for 30–60 minutes before cooking. Drain, then drop into a saucepan of boiling water and cook for 6–10 minutes, testing every minute after the first 6 minutes so you will know when they are done. As soon as they are tender, drain in a colander and rinse well in cold running water. Drain once more. They can then be fried or heated in soup before serving.

Dried rice vermicelli (rice-stick) noodles: Rice vermicelli has very fine strands and cooks very quickly. Drop into boiling water and cook for 2–3 minutes only. Drain well. Serve in soups or with dishes that have a good amount of sauce. Or, if a crisp garnish is required, use rice vermicelli straight from the packet and deep-fry small amounts for just a few seconds. It will puff and become white as soon as it is immersed in the oil if it is hot enough. Lift out quickly on a slotted spoon or wire strainer and drain on paper towels before serving.

Dried cellophane (bean thread) noodles: Also known as bean starch noodles, these dried noodles need to be soaked in hot water for 20 minutes, then drained and cooked in a saucepan of boiling water for 15 minutes, or until tender. For use as a crisp garnish, deep-fry them in hot oil straight from the packet, as for rice vermicelli (above). In Japan they have a similar fine translucent noodle, known as harusame.

Preparing soft-fried noodles

After the noodles have been boiled and drained, spread them on a large baking tray lined with paper towel and leave them to dry for at least 30 minutes – a little peanut oil may be sprinkled over them to prevent sticking. Heat 2 tablespoons each of peanut oil and sesame oil in a wok or large heavy-based frying pan until hot, then add a handful of noodles and cook until golden on one side. Turn and cook the other side until golden, then remove to a plate. Repeat with the remaining noodles. It may be necessary to add more oil to the wok if a large quantity of noodles is being fried, but make sure the fresh oil is very hot first. Serve with beef, pork, poultry or vegetable dishes.

Preparing crisp-fried noodles

Rice vermicelli (rice-stick) and cellophane (bean thread) noodles can be fried in hot oil straight from the packet. Egg noodles need to be cooked first, then drained and spread out on a large baking tray lined with paper towel to dry for at least 30 minutes – a little peanut oil can be sprinkled over them to prevent sticking. Heat sufficient peanut oil in a wok or heavy-based frying pan over medium heat. When the oil is hot, deep-fry the noodles, in batches, until crisp and golden brown. Drain on paper towel. These crisp noodles are used mainly as a garnish.

Preparing whole chickens

Jointing a chicken

I have often referred to cutting a chicken into serving pieces suitable for a curry. This is simply cutting the pieces smaller than joints so that the spices can more readily penetrate and flavour the meat.

To joint a chicken, first cut off the thighs and drumsticks, then separate the drumsticks from the thighs. Cut off the wings and divide them at the middle joint (wing tips may be added to a stock but do not count as a joint). The breast is divided down the centre into two, then across into four pieces – do not start cooking the breast pieces at the same time as the others, but add them later, as breast meat has a tendency to become dry if cooked for too long.

A 1.5 kg (3 lb 5 oz) chicken, for instance, can be jointed, then broken down further into serving pieces. The thighs are cut into two with a heavy cleaver; the back is cut into four pieces and used in the curry, though not counted as serving pieces because there is very little meat on them. Neck and giblets are also included to give extra flavour.

Preparing whole fish

Cutting fish fillets into serving pieces

Fish fillets are of varying thickness, length and density. For example, whole fillets of flathead can be dipped in batter and will cook in less than a minute in hot oil, whereas a fillet of ling or trevalla will need to be cut into 3 cm (1¼ in) strips for the same recipe.

Let common sense prevail when portioning fish fillets, but always remember that fish is cooked when the flesh turns opaque when flaked with a fork or knife.

Cutting fish steaks into serving pieces

Depending on the size of the fish, each steak may need to be cut into four, six or eight pieces. Once again, smaller portions are better, for they allow flavours to penetrate and you can allow more than one piece per person. The accompanying sketch shows how to divide fish steaks – small ones into four pieces, medium-sized ones into six pieces and really large steaks into eight pieces.

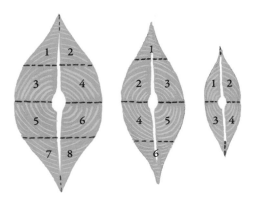

Indonesia

From the air, the Indonesian archipelago is like a beautiful necklace of aquamarine, sapphire and emerald hues, strung between Australia and mainland Southeast Asia. Of its more than 13,000 islands, only half are large enough to have names and less than a thousand are populated, yet it includes some of the world's largest islands and is home to more than 245 million people, making it the fourth most populous nation on earth.

On the ground it is green, green, green. The steamy heat of the lowlands and the lush growth suggest that one is in a giant greenhouse, a notion that holds true for all but the chilly mountain peaks and high volcanic craters that are the backbones of most of the major islands. Indonesia has, at various times, been in the thrall of animism, Buddhism, Hinduism and Islam. It has been influenced or conquered by the Chinese, the Indians, the Portuguese, the Dutch and the English. It had huge and magnificent temples centuries before Europe's great gothic cathedrals were dreamed of. Its handcrafts and theatre – batik and the famed *wayang kulit* or 'shadow plays' – are as alive today as they were a thousand years ago.

This rich and varied history, coupled with many different traditions and languages, has inevitably produced a cuisine that is also rich and varied – and which offers much to the adventurous eater.

Indonesian food is, unquestionably, some of the most delicious in the world. There isn't much subtlety about it, but what a great awakening for your taste buds! This doesn't mean that every dish is hot or pungent, but there's always a combination of sweet and sour and salty tastes; unexpectedly gentle sauces of coconut milk fragrant with lemongrass or other herbs; crisp textured accompaniments; hot sambals to be tasted in tiny quantities; all of which create an awareness that what you are eating is not just body fuel but an expression of culinary artistry.

One of the simplest, most unsophisticated Indonesian meals I have eaten was at an open-air restaurant in Jakarta. Near the entrance were tables laden with enormous piles of tender coconuts and spiky, strong-smelling durian; from beams in the little thatched shelter hung strings of purple mangosteens, mangoes, rambutan and other exotic fruit. At this restaurant the speciality was fish. And fish there were, all around. Paths wound between ponds well stocked with varieties of fish considered delicacies in Indonesia. The water was recirculated by means of fountains in the ponds. Pavilions open on all sides dotted the grounds and here one sat at bare tables. Before sitting down we chose our fish, pointing them out to the men who waded in, net in hand, to capture our dinner.

The meal, when it came, was extremely simple. There was a whole fish to each person; some had been deep-fried, others barbecued. To accompany the fish was a basket filled with steaming white rice. Each diner had a bowl of soup, very light and clear, but full of the unusual flavours of acid with tamarind and sweet with the natural sugars of vegetables like corn and pumpkin (winter squash) – this was for sipping between mouthfuls of food, not for downing as a first course. There was a salad of cucumber spears and other vegetables and fresh green leaves far more intriguing than lettuce; even tender papaya leaves were included. Each of us had a small stone dish of freshly ground chilli sambal with a stone pestle-like spoon resting in it. This was the dynamite that set the whole meal apart and assured us that we were dining in Indonesia. The fish was delightful – fried or barbecued, the flesh was moist and delicate, the small bones so crisply cooked that they crunched and melted. To take care of the big bones there were numerous friendly and well-fed cats (it was considered quite in order to throw the bones to the feline clientele).

To drink, we had young coconuts with the top cut off, a dash of orange-flavoured syrup and crushed ice added to the water inside. For dessert we were deluged with fresh green-skinned citrus fruits of amazing sweetness and a whole string of mangosteens – gentle pressure between the palms cracks open the thick purple shell to disclose a number of milky white segments like those in a mandarin, but with no covering membrane or little seeds. Their sweet-sour, slightly astringent, refreshing flavour makes you eat another and yet another until there is a tell-tale heap of purple shells before you.

Indonesian sweets are mostly made from glutinous rice, but don't shrug them off with thoughts of rice pudding – there's not the slightest resemblance. The rice might be steamed in tiny baskets woven of fresh leaves, sweetened with palm sugar (jaggery), flavoured with fragrant leaves and flowers; or it might be ground and cooked with coconut milk to a smooth paste, flavoured and coloured and poured in unbelievably fine alternate layers of white and green or pink or yellow or chocolate.

Serving and eating an Indonesian meal

Whatever else is served, rice is always the foundation of an Indonesian meal. Cook your rice by the absorption method or by steaming; it has so much more flavour than rice cooked in water and drained, and it also has the correct texture and pearly appearance. With rice it is customary to serve a fish curry and a poultry or meat curry, or both; two or more vegetable dishes, one a *sayur* with lots of gravy, and at least one other vegetable, stir-fried, boiled or served as a salad. Accompaniments such as krupuk and chilli-based condiments are an integral part of the meal.

The word 'sambal' implies something fried with lots of chillies. It doesn't only include high-powered condiments such as sambal ulek or sambal bajak, which are basically pastes of ground chilli and other seasonings; it can also mean one or more of several main dishes known as *sambal sambalan* – there are prawn (shrimp) sambals, chicken sambals, beef sambals – so you could accompany your rice with a generous helping of Sambal cumi-cumi pedis (page 50) and a tiny accent of Sambal bajak (page 112).

Most popular Indonesian sambal pastes or condiments are available in Western countries. Making them involves handling large quantities of fresh chillies and this can be an unforgettable experience if one is in the least bit careless. I recommend buying these sambals in bottles. They are eaten or used in recipes in such tiny quantities that it is hardly worth the trouble to make them. Store bottles in the refrigerator after opening and use a dry spoon, and they'll keep well. There are some recipes for those who find it impossible to buy the sambals.

Because Indonesian cookery never gets very far without fresh chillies, have disposable gloves ready and use them when handling any kind of chilli. If you do forget and touch the chillies, keep your hands away from your eyes, your face and delicate skin. Washing well with soap and water helps, but don't be surprised if the more pungent chillies cause a tingling and burning sensation that goes on for hours. When planning an Indonesian meal, the curries can be prepared a day or two before and refrigerated – they usually develop more flavour with keeping. Accompaniments can also be made earlier in the day and chilled, or heated up at the last minute if they are to be served hot. Soups and vegetables (*sayur*) can be made in advance too, but short-cook the dish so that the final re-heating will not result in the vegetables being overcooked.

For a rice meal set the table with a plate, dessert spoon, fork and a bowl for soup. Everything is put on the table at the same time except sweets or fruits. Rice is taken first and should be surrounded by small helpings of curries and other accompaniments, which are mixed with the rice either singly or in combination.

It is quite polite to eat an Indonesian meal with one's fingers, as most Indonesians do, but practise without an audience first; there's quite an art to doing it properly. Only the tips of the fingers of the right hand are used. When soups and *sayur* are part of the meal a spoon proves more convenient. Fingerbowls are provided, with slices of lemon or lime floating in hot water.

Utensils

The range of saucepans, knives and spoons already in the kitchen will do very well for cooking Indonesian food, but there is one pan that will make things a lot easier. This is the curved metal pan with a shallow bowl-like shape known to most of us as a wok, but called a *kuali* or *wajan*. Woks are readily available and are inexpensive (see information on the wok on pages 7–8). In most Indonesian kitchens, grinding stones are part of the essential equipment, as is a stone mortar and pestle. You can buy a mortar and pestle for pounding small amounts of spices, or invest in an electric spice grinder. To substitute for the grinding stone you need a powerful blender. I would stress that some do a better job than others. Mine has a glass goblet, a powerful motor and a shape that will effectively blend small quantities as well as large. I use it all the time for grinding spices, pulverising onions, chillies, garlic and ginger, making coconut milk and a number of other tasks.

In Asian kitchens you will find a special implement for grating fresh coconut, but rather than try to grate the coconut with an ordinary grater, peel away the dark brown outer skin and pulverise the coconut in a food processor or blender. Frozen grated coconut is available from Indian grocery stores.

On the subject of graters, I have often recommended using grated ginger or garlic. This is because it is the nearest you can come to the ground ingredient and because most blenders need more than a couple of cloves of garlic or a fragment of ginger to work on – but please choose the right grater surface – not the one for grating cheese or the larger shredder, but the small version of the shredder. This gives a very satisfactory result.

Your Indonesian shelf

This is a list of spices, sauces, sambals and other flavourings which are often used in Indonesian cooking and good to have on hand to make the recipes in this chapter.

candlenuts or brazil nuts

coconut, desiccated (shredded) or freshly grated

coconut cream and milk (pages 8–9)

coriander, ground

cumin, ground

curry leaves

daun salam leaves

dried shrimp

dried shrimp paste

galangal, fresh or brined

glutinous rice (ketan)

kecap manis (sweet dark soy sauce) or use dark soy sauce

kencur (aromatic ginger) powder

laos (dried galangal) powder

palm sugar (jaggery), or use soft or dark brown sugar

pandanus leaves

peanut oil

salted soy beans (taucheo)

sambal bajak (page 112)

sambal ulek (page 104)

sereh powder (dried ground lemongrass)

sesame oil

shrimp sauce

soy sauce

tamarind pulp

turmeric, ground

Note

Though fresh galangal may look similar to ginger, this rhizome is infinitely harder to cut. Sliced, it adds flavour simply by simmering in soups and sauces, but for a curry paste, the rhizome will need to be peeled and finely chopped before grinding with a mortar and pestle with other ingredients. If you do not have access to the fresh root, sliced galangal in brine is the next best option. Otherwise, use the dry ground spice, known as laos powder. It will imbue the food with the correct flavour note, though perhaps with a little less of the lively zing delivered by the fresh rhizome.

Rice
and
Noodles

❁

Nasi Putih
White rice

Serves: 6

....

495 g (1 lb 1 oz/2¼ cups) short-grain rice

2 teaspoons salt (optional)

Variation

For long-grain rice, use 1 litre (34 fl oz/4 cups) water to 495 g (1 lb 1 oz/2½ cups) rice, for the absorption rate is almost double that of short- or medium-grain rice. Use the same method of cooking, bringing rice and water to the boil and then covering and reducing the heat so that it cooks very gently. Increase the cooking time to 20 minutes after the rice comes to the boil.

Wash the rice well and drain in a colander for 30 minutes. Put the rice into a saucepan with a tight-fitting lid. Add 625 ml (21 fl oz/2½ cups) water and the salt, if using, and bring to the boil. As soon as it comes to the boil, reduce the heat to low, cover, and allow to steam for 15 minutes. This gives a very firm rice, which can be eaten hot or allowed to get cold and used for Nasi goreng (page 21).

(Though firm, rice will be cooked through if the lid is put on as soon as the rice comes to the boil, and if the lid fits well enough to hold the steam in. It is also possible to bring water and salt to the boil, add the rice and when it returns to the boil, cover and steam as before.) A most important point when cooking rice is that the lid should not be lifted during cooking time, as valuable steam is lost and can affect the result. Also, rice is never stirred during cooking.

If a slightly softer result is preferred (but with each grain separate and not mushy) increase the water to 750 ml (25½ fl oz/3 cups).

Nasi Uduk
Rice cooked in coconut milk with spices

Serves: 6

500 g (1 lb 2 oz/2½ cups) long-grain rice

1.1 litres (37 fl oz/4½ cups) thin coconut milk
(pages 8–9)

2½ teaspoons salt

1 onion, finely chopped

2 garlic cloves, finely chopped

1 teaspoon ground turmeric

1 teaspoon ground cumin

2 teaspoons ground coriander

½ teaspoon dried shrimp paste

¼ teaspoon kencur (aromatic ginger) powder

1 stem lemongrass or 1 teaspoon finely grated
lemon zest

Wash the rice well and drain in a colander for 30 minutes.

Put all the ingredients, except the rice, into a saucepan with a tight-fitting lid, and bring slowly to the boil, stirring frequently. Add the rice, stir and bring back to the boil, then reduce the heat to low, cover, and steam for 20 minutes.

Uncover, use a fork to lightly pull the rice from the side of the pan, mixing in any coconut milk that has not been absorbed, then replace the lid and steam for 5 minutes further. Serve hot with Ayam goreng jawa (page 56) and sambals.

Nasi Gurih
Fragrant rice

Serves: 6

500 g (1 lb 2 oz/2½ cups) long-grain rice

1.1 litres (37 fl oz/4½ cups) coconut milk
(pages 8–9)

½ teaspoon freshly ground black pepper

1 stem lemongrass or 1 teaspoon finely grated
lemon zest

½ teaspoon freshly grated nutmeg or
ground mace

¼ teaspoon ground cloves

6 daun salam leaves (glossary)

2½ teaspoons salt

Wash the rice well and drain in a colander for 30 minutes.

Put all the ingredients, except the rice, into a saucepan with a tight-fitting lid, and bring slowly to the boil, stirring frequently. Add the rice, stir and bring back to the boil, then reduce the heat to low, cover, and steam for 20 minutes.

Uncover, use a fork to lightly pull the rice from the side of the pan, mixing in any coconut milk that has not been absorbed, then replace the lid and steam for 5 minutes further. Serve hot with fried chicken or curries and hot sambals.

Nasi Goreng
Fried rice

Serves: 6–8

3 eggs

salt and freshly ground black pepper, to taste

oil for frying

2 onions, chopped

2 garlic cloves, chopped

½ teaspoon dried shrimp paste

250 g (9 oz) raw small prawns (shrimp), peeled and deveined

500 g (1 lb 2 oz) pork or lean beef steak, thinly sliced

740 g (1 lb 10 oz/4 cups) cold cooked rice

6 spring onions (scallions), thinly sliced

2 tablespoons light soy sauce

3 tablespoons Fried onion flakes (page 105), to garnish

1 Lebanese (short) cucumber, thinly sliced, to garnish

Beat the eggs in a bowl; season with salt and freshly ground black pepper, to taste. Heat a little of the oil in a frying pan over low heat. Pour in half of the egg to make an omelette, then remove to a plate to cool; do not fold the omelette. Repeat with the remaining egg. When cool, put one omelette on top of the other, roll up and cut into thin strips. Set aside.

Put the onion, garlic and shrimp paste in a food processor and process to make a paste. Alternatively, finely chop the onion and crush the garlic. Dissolve the shrimp paste in a little hot water and combine with the onion and garlic.

Heat 3 tablespoons of the oil in a wok or large heavy-based frying pan over medium heat. Add the onion mixture and cook until aromatic. Add the prawns and pork and stir-fry until cooked through. Add another 2 tablespoons of the oil and when hot, stir in the cooked rice and spring onion, tossing until well combined and very hot. Add the soy sauce and mix well to combine. Serve the fried rice garnished with strips of omelette, the onion flakes and cucumber.

Mie Goreng
Fried noodles

Serves: 4

250 g (9 oz) fresh or dried fine egg noodles

80 ml (2½ fl oz/⅓ cup) peanut oil

1 onion, finely chopped

3 garlic cloves, finely chopped

1 fresh red chilli, deseeded and sliced

½ teaspoon dried shrimp paste

1 large pork chop, trimmed of fat and diced

250 g (9 oz) raw small prawns (shrimp),
   peeled and deveined

2 celery stalks, thinly sliced

1 small wedge of cabbage, finely shredded

1 teaspoon salt

½ teaspoon freshly ground black pepper

1–2 tablespoons light soy sauce

Fried onion flakes (page 105) (optional),
   to garnish

4 spring onions (scallions), thinly sliced,
   to garnish

1 Lebanese (short) cucumber, thinly sliced,
   to garnish

Soak the noodles in hot water and drain. Cook the noodles in a saucepan of boiling water until tender, then refresh immediately under cold running water and drain well.

Heat the peanut oil in a wok or large heavy-based frying pan over medium heat. Add the onion, garlic and chilli and stir-fry until the onion is soft and starts to turn golden. Add the shrimp paste, pork and prawns and stir-fry until cooked through. Add the celery, cabbage, salt and pepper and stir-fry for a further 1–2 minutes, or until just tender – the vegetables should still be crisp.

Add the noodles and keep tossing the mixture so that every part of it gets heated through. Add the soy sauce, to taste. Pile into a serving dish and sprinkle over the onion flakes, if using, spring onion and cucumber. Serve hot.

Nasi Kuning Lengkap
Festive yellow rice

Serves: 8–10

1 kg (2 lb 3 oz/5 cups) long-grain rice

80 ml (2½ fl oz/⅓ cup) oil

2 large onions, thinly sliced

3 garlic cloves, finely chopped

2 litres (68 fl oz/8 cups) coconut milk
(pages 8–9)

1 tablespoon salt

2 teaspoons ground turmeric

6 dried daun salam leaves (glossary) or
2 pandanus leaves

banana leaves or bamboo leaves, to serve

Indonesian marbled eggs (page 104),
peeled and halved, to garnish

2 Lebanese (short) cucumbers, thinly sliced

3 fresh red chillies, deseeded and
thinly sliced

3 fresh green chillies, deseeded and
thinly sliced

Accompaniments

Javanese-style fried chicken (page 56)

Piquant fried prawn sambal (page 103)

Meat and coconut patties (page 82)

Crisp spiced coconut with peanuts
(page 111)

Vegetable pickle (page 152)

Prawn crisps (page 31)

Peanut wafers (page 30)

Wash the rice well and drain in a colander for 30 minutes.

Heat the oil in a large saucepan with a tight-fitting lid over low heat. Add the onion and garlic and cook until the onion is soft and golden. Add the rice and cook for 1–2 minutes, then add the coconut milk, salt, turmeric and daun salam leaves. Bring to the boil, stirring with a wooden spoon. As soon as the liquid starts to boil, reduce the heat to low, cover, and steam for 20 minutes. Uncover, use a fork to quickly stir in any coconut milk from the edge of the pan, then replace the lid and continue cooking over low heat for a further 3 minutes. Remove from the heat, uncover, and allow to cool slightly. Remove the daun salam leaves and gently fork the rice onto a large platter or a tray lined with well-washed banana or bamboo leaves. Shape into a cone, pressing firmly – you can use pieces of greased banana leaf or foil to do this. Arrange the marbled eggs, cucumber and chilli around the base and serve with the accompaniments as listed opposite.

Note

For a traditional decorative effect, make a flower with one of the red chillies. To do this, scrape out the seeds with the point of a sharp knife, then cut off the stem end and make several slits from 2.5 cm (1 in) above the tip to the stem end. Drop into iced water and the strips will curl. Put this on top of the cone, scatter the sliced chillies around the side of the cone, and put the sliced cucumbers and marbled eggs around the base of the cone.

Soups
and
Snacks

❀

Lemper
Rice rolls with spicy filling

Wrapping food in banana leaves is a very popular method of cooking and serving in Southeast Asia. Where banana leaves are available, prepare them by stripping the leaves from the thick middle rib with a sharp knife. Leaves will be inclined to split, but this doesn't matter, as they will have to be cut into suitable sizes for serving anyway. Wash the leaves to remove any dust, then pour boiling water over them. This makes them pliable enough to fold without splitting. Ti leaves or bamboo leaves (from Chinese grocery stores) can be used instead of banana leaves, but heavy-duty foil does the job efficiently even if it isn't as picturesque. These rolls are ideal for picnics or buffet parties.

500 g (1 lb 2 oz/2¼ cups) glutinous rice (ketan)

250 ml (8½ fl oz/1 cup) thick coconut milk (pages 8–9)

250 g (9 oz) minced (ground) pork or diced chicken

½ teaspoon salt

½ teaspoon freshly ground black pepper

2 tablespoons oil

2 garlic cloves, crushed

4 dried daun salam leaves (glossary)

2 teaspoons ground coriander

1 teaspoon ground cumin

½ teaspoon ground turmeric

½ teaspoon dried shrimp paste

a squeeze of lemon juice

banana leaf or aluminium foil

Wash the rice well and drain in a colander for 30 minutes.

Put the rice into a saucepan with 500 ml (17 fl oz/2 cups) water and bring to the boil, then reduce the heat to low, cover, and steam for 15 minutes.

Mix 190 ml (6½ fl oz/¾ cup) of the coconut milk with 125 ml (4 fl oz/½ cup) water in a small saucepan and heat without boiling. Add to the rice, stir gently with a fork, cover and steam for a further 5–10 minutes, or until the coconut milk has been absorbed. Remove from the heat and allow to cool.

Season the pork with the salt and pepper. Heat the oil in a wok or heavy-based frying pan over low heat. Add the garlic and daun salam leaves and cook for 1 minute, then add the ground spices and shrimp paste and stir-fry for 1 minute, crushing the shrimp paste with a spoon. Add the pork and cook until the colour changes. Add the remaining coconut milk and simmer over low heat until well cooked and quite dry. Add the lemon juice and season with salt and pepper to taste. Remove from the heat and allow to cool.

Take a large tablespoonful of the rice and flatten on a piece of banana leaf. Put a good teaspoonful of the filling in the middle and mould the rice around it to make a cylindrical shape. Roll the banana leaf and secure with wooden toothpicks, or roll in the foil to make a neat parcel. These parcels can be heated over a barbecue or steamed for 15 minutes, then allowed to cool once again. Serve at room temperature as a snack.

Soups and Snacks ❖

Pilus
Fried sweet potato balls

Makes: 20

500 g (1 lb 2 oz) sweet potatoes, peeled and chopped

1 tablespoon chopped dark palm sugar (jaggery)

1–2 tablespoons ground rice

oil for frying

Put the sweet potato into a saucepan with enough water to cover and bring to the boil. Cook until tender but not mushy. Drain well, then mash until quite smooth. Add the palm sugar and enough of the ground rice to make the mixture firm enough to mould. Take 1 tablespoon of the mixture at a time and roll it into small balls, the size of a large marble.

Heat the oil in a wok or large heavy-based saucepan over medium heat. When the oil is hot, deep-fry the balls, in batches, until golden brown all over. Remove with a slotted spoon and drain on paper towel. Serve plain or with sugar syrup and fresh grated coconut as a snack.

Rempeyek Udang
Prawn fritters

Makes: 18–22

2 eggs, beaten

1 tablespoon rice flour

2 tablespoons ground rice

1 small garlic clove, crushed

¾ teaspoon salt

¼ teaspoon freshly ground black pepper

¼ teaspoon kencur (aromatic ginger) powder

¼ teaspoon sereh powder (dried ground lemongrass) (optional)

1 fresh red chilli, deseeded and sliced

1 small onion, thinly sliced

250 g (9 oz) raw prawns (shrimp), peeled, deveined and chopped

peanut oil for deep-frying

Combine the egg, rice flour, ground rice, garlic, salt, pepper, kencur powder, sereh powder, if using, and 1 tablespoon water in a mixing bowl. Fold in the chilli, onion and prawns and stir well to combine.

Heat the peanut oil in a wok or large heavy-based saucepan over medium heat. Take 1 large tablespoon of the mixture at a time and lower it into the hot oil. Deep-fry the fritters, in batches, until golden brown on both sides. Remove from the pan and drain on paper towel placed on a wire rack – this will keep the fritters crisp. Repeat until all the mixture is cooked, then serve hot.

Soups and Snacks

Pergedel Jagung
Corn fritters

Makes: 12–14

---

75 g (2¾ oz/½ cup) plain (all-purpose) flour

80 g (2¾ oz/½ cup) ground rice

¼ teaspoon baking powder

½ teaspoon salt

1 teaspoon ground coriander

1 teaspoon ground cumin

½ teaspoon laos (dried galangal) powder (optional)

1 teaspoon chilli powder (optional)

1 egg, beaten

½ teaspoon dried shrimp paste (optional)

a squeeze of lemon juice

500 g (1 lb 2 oz/2½ cups) corn kernels

1 onion, thinly sliced

1 garlic clove, crushed with a pinch of salt

1 celery stalk, diced

oil for frying

Sift the flour, ground rice and baking powder into a bowl and add the salt, coriander, cumin, laos powder and chilli powder, if using.

In a separate bowl, mix together the egg, shrimp paste, if using, lemon juice and 250 ml (8½ fl oz/1 cup) water. Add to the flour mixture, beating until smooth. Stir in the corn, onion, garlic and celery until well combined.

Heat the oil in a wok or large heavy-based frying pan over medium heat. Drop 1 large tablespoon of the mixture at a time into the hot oil, spreading it with the back of the spoon to make a circle shape with a 7.5 cm (3 in) diameter. Cook until the fritter is golden brown on one side, then turn and cook the other side until golden. Remove from the pan and drain on paper towel placed on a wire rack – this will keep the fritters crisp. Repeat until all the mixture is cooked, then serve hot.

Note

Without the chilli powder and shrimp paste the fritters are milder in flavour, but if you like a little excitement in the flavouring add them. Ground rice adds crispness.

Rempeyek Kacang
Peanut wafers

Makes: 24

An accompaniment to rice and curries on festive occasions, these crisp and crunchy wafers are also delicious served by themselves as a snack or as an accompaniment to drinks. Toast the raw peanuts in a 180°C (350°F) oven for 30–35 minutes, and rub the skins off before using.

90 g (3 oz/½ cup) rice flour

2 tablespoons ground rice

1 teaspoon ground coriander

½ teaspoon ground cumin

¼ teaspoon ground turmeric

¼ teaspoon kencur (aromatic ginger) powder (optional)

¾ teaspoon salt

250 ml (8½ fl oz/1 cup) coconut milk (pages 8–9)

1 garlic clove, crushed

1 small onion, finely chopped

120 g (4½ oz/¾ cup) roasted, unsalted peanuts

oil for frying

Sift the rice flour and ground rice into a bowl and add the coriander, cumin, turmeric, kencur powder, if using, and salt. Add the coconut milk and beat to make a smooth thin batter. Add the garlic, onion and peanuts and stir to combine.

Pour the oil into a large frying pan to a depth of 1 cm (½ in). When the oil is hot, drop 1 tablespoon of the batter mixture into the oil at a time – the batter should be thin enough to spread into a lacy wafer. (If it holds together and has to be spread with the spoon, it is too thick, and must be thinned by adding a spoonful of coconut milk at a time until the correct consistency is obtained.) Cook the wafers until golden brown on one side, then turn over and cook until golden. Remove from the pan and drain on paper towel placed on a wire rack – this will keep the wafers crisp. Repeat with the remaining mixture until it is all cooked. Cool and store in an airtight container.

Variation

To make coconut wafers proceed as for peanut wafers (above), but omit the peanuts and add 65 g (2¼ oz/¾ cup) freshly grated coconut or 90 g (3 oz/1 cup) desiccated (shredded) coconut.

Krupuk Udang
Prawn crisps

These come in various shapes, sizes and colours, but the most flavoursome are the large, salmon-pink variety roughly as long as the average hand and half as wide. They cost more than other types, but more than compensate because of their distinct prawn (shrimp) flavour. Made from a starch base and ground prawns, they need to be fried in deep hot oil to become light, crisp, crunchy and swell to more than double their original size.

Sometimes prawn crisps become damp due to climatic conditions, and do not puff as they should when fried. It is a good precaution to dry them out in a low oven for 10–15 minutes, spread out in a single layer on a baking tray. Let them cool, then store in an airtight container. Or dry them out in the oven as required just before cooking.

oil for frying

dried prawn (shrimp) crisp wafers

Heat the oil in a wok or large heavy-based frying pan over medium heat. When the oil is hot, add the larger wafers one at a time, spooning oil over them as they cook – the oil should be hot enough to make them swell within 2–3 seconds of being dropped in. Test with a small piece first. If the oil is not the right temperature they will be tough and leathery, not crisp and melting. On the other hand if the oil is too hot they will brown too fast. A little practice will tell how hot the oil should be.

Remove the wafers with a slotted spoon and drain on paper towel (placed on a wire rack – this will keep the wafers crisp). Cool thoroughly before storing in an airtight container. Once cooked they will keep for up to 4 days.

Terung Lodeh
Prawn and eggplant soup

Serves: 4

1 tablespoon dried shrimp or 125 g (4½ oz)
    raw prawns (shrimp), peeled, deveined
    and chopped

2 tablespoons peanut oil

1 onion, finely chopped

2 garlic cloves, finely chopped

2 fresh red chillies, deseeded and chopped

1 ripe tomato, peeled and chopped

4 dried daun salam leaves (glossary)

500 ml (17 fl oz/2 cups) chicken stock

1 eggplant (aubergine), peeled and diced

250 ml (8½ fl oz/1 cup) coconut milk
    (pages 8–9)

½ teaspoon soft brown sugar (optional)

1 teaspoon salt, or to taste

If using dried shrimp, place it in a bowl with 125 ml (4 fl oz/½ cup) hot water and leave to soak for 10 minutes.

Heat the oil in a large saucepan over low heat. Add the onion, garlic and chilli and cook until the onion is soft and golden. Add the tomato and daun salam leaves and cook for 5 minutes, mashing the tomato to a pulp. Add the stock and dried shrimp, if using, and bring to the boil, then reduce the heat. Add the eggplant and simmer for about 10–15 minutes, or until just tender. Add the coconut milk, fresh prawns and sugar, if using, and the salt and stir while heating through – the fresh prawns will turn opaque when cooked. Taste and add more salt if necessary. Serve with rice and curries.

Soto Ayam (1)
Chicken soup (delicate)

Serves: 6

1.5 kg (3 lb 5 oz) whole chicken

2 teaspoons salt

3 whole black peppercorns

1 celery stalk

1 small onion

2 slices fresh ginger, bruised

2 garlic cloves, bruised

60 g (2 oz) cellophane (bean thread) noodles

135 g (5 oz/1½ cups) fresh bean sprouts, trimmed

2 hard-boiled eggs, peeled and chopped, to garnish

2 spring onions (scallions), thinly sliced, to garnish

Joint the chicken (see page 13) and put into a large saucepan with enough cold water to cover and add the salt, peppercorns, celery, onion, ginger and garlic. Bring to the boil, then reduce the heat to low, cover, and simmer for 35–45 minutes. Cool, then strain into a bowl. Remove and discard the skin and bones from the chicken and finely chop the meat. Set aside.

Meanwhile, soak the cellophane noodles in hot water for 20 minutes and drain. Cook the noodles according to the packet instructions. Drain well and cut into short lengths.

Just before serving, put the chicken broth and meat into a clean saucepan over medium–high heat and add the noodles, stirring until warmed through; adjust the seasoning, to taste.

Put the bean sprouts into individual soup bowls and pour the boiling broth over the top. Garnish with the egg and spring onion and serve at once.

Soto Ayam (2)
Chicken soup (very spicy)

Serves: 6

1.5 kg (3 lb 5 oz) whole chicken

3 teaspoons salt

½ teaspoon whole black peppercorns

3–4 sprigs celery leaves

2 onions, 1 left whole, 1 thinly sliced

2 tablespoons peanut oil

2 fresh red chillies, deseeded and chopped

10 dried daun salam leaves (glossary)

2 garlic cloves, crushed

1 teaspoon finely grated fresh ginger

1 teaspoon dried shrimp paste

1 teaspoon ground turmeric

1½ tablespoons ground coriander

2 teaspoons ground cumin

½ teaspoon ground fennel

½ teaspoon freshly ground black pepper

½ teaspoon freshly grated nutmeg

lemon juice, to taste

100 g (3½ oz) dried fine egg noodles

Garnish

3 hard-boiled eggs, peeled and chopped

6 garlic cloves, sliced and fried (see note)

8 spring onions (scallions), thinly sliced

Fried onion flakes (page 105)

fried dried chillies (see note)

crumbled potato chips (crisps)

Sambal bajak (page 112) or Sambal ulek
  (page 104)

Joint the chicken (see page 13) and put into a large saucepan with 2 litres (68 fl oz/8 cups) water. Add the salt, peppercorns, celery leaves and the whole onion. Bring to the boil, then reduce the heat to low, cover, and simmer for 35–40 minutes, or until the chicken is tender. Cool, then strain and reserve the stock. Remove and discard the skin and bones from the chicken and finely chop the meat. Set aside.

Heat the peanut oil in a large saucepan over low heat. Add the sliced onion, chilli and daun salam leaves and cook until the onion is soft and starts to brown. Add the garlic, ginger and shrimp paste and stir-fry, crushing the shrimp paste with a spoon. Add all the ground spices and fry for a few seconds longer. Add the strained stock and bring to the boil, then reduce the heat, cover, and simmer for 10 minutes. Stir in the lemon juice.

Soak the egg noodles in hot water, then drain and cook in boiling water until tender. Drain well and add to the soup with the chicken meat. Serve the soup hot, garnished with the egg, fried garlic, spring onion and fried onion flakes. Serve the dried chilli, potato chips and sambal in separate bowls to be added to individual servings, according to taste. Sambals should be added in very small amounts and only by those who know what to expect and who like their soup fiery hot.

Note

To fry garlic, peel the cloves and cut into slices of equal thickness. Deep-fry in oil over low heat just until the garlic turns pale golden. Remove from the oil immediately and drain on paper towel – do not let the colour darken too much or the garlic will have a bitter taste. Dry chillies only need a few seconds of frying until done.

Fish and Seafood

❀

Tauco Ikan

Fish in brown bean sauce with stir-fried vegetables

Serves: 6

750 g (1 lb 11 oz) fish steaks, such as tuna, mackerel or jewfish

80 ml (2½ fl oz/⅓ cup) peanut oil

2 small onions, 1 finely chopped, 1 chopped into large pieces

1½ teaspoons finely grated fresh ginger

2 garlic cloves, finely chopped

2 tablespoons salted soy beans (taucheo), drained

1 teaspoon dried shrimp paste (optional)

6 banana chillies or 1 red capsicum (bell pepper), deseeded and sliced

125 g (4½ oz/1 cup) sliced green beans

250 g (9 oz/1 cup) sliced bamboo shoots

1 tablespoon light soy sauce

Wipe the fish with damp paper towel. Cut the fish into serving portions (see page 13). Season with salt.

Heat the peanut oil in a wok or large heavy-based frying pan over high heat. Cook the fish on both sides until golden. Remove to a plate.

Pour off all but 2 tablespoons of the oil and place the wok over medium heat. Add the finely chopped onion, ginger, garlic and salted soy beans and cook, stirring constantly, until the onion is soft. Add the shrimp paste, if using, and stir-fry for 2 minutes, then add the chilli and remaining onion and stir-fry for 1 minute further. Add the bamboo shoots, soy sauce and 170 ml (5½ fl oz/⅔ cup) water, stir well, cover, and simmer for 3 minutes. Return the fish to the pan and heat through. Serve with white rice.

Note

Instead of frying the fish in oil, you can add it to the pan after the water has been added and starts to simmer, then cover the pan and cook the fish for 6–8 minutes, depending on the thickness of the fish. In this case, only 2 tablespoons of oil will be necessary.

Ikan Panggang (1)
Fish grilled in banana leaves

Serves: 4

4 small whole fish, cleaned and scaled (head left on) or 4 fish steaks

2 garlic cloves

3 teaspoons chopped dark palm sugar (jaggery)

2 fresh red chillies, deseeded and chopped

125 ml (4 fl oz/½ cup) dark soy sauce

1 tablespoon lemon juice

½ teaspoon kencur (aromatic ginger) powder

4 squares banana leaf and foil

2 lemons, thinly sliced

Wipe the fish with damp paper towel. If using whole fish, rub salt over the body and make diagonal cuts on each side.

Crush the garlic with some of the palm sugar. Combine the garlic, palm sugar, chilli, soy sauce, lemon juice and kencur powder in a bowl and stir well to combine. Pour over the fish in a shallow non-reactive dish and leave to marinate for 30 minutes.

Drain well, reserving the marinade. Place each fish (or each fish steak) on a square of banana leaf backed with a layer of foil. Pour one spoonful of the marinade inside and over the top of the fish. Put a few lemon slices on top, overlapping them slightly, and then wrap up the parcel to enclose the fish.

Cook the fish, seam side up, over glowing coals or under a preheated grill (broiler) for 10 minutes on each side, or until cooked through.

Meanwhile, put the remaining marinade in a saucepan over low heat and simmer for 2–3 minutes, adding more soy sauce and water if necessary. Serve the fish in their parcels with the marinade sauce on the side. Serve with rice, vegetables and sambals.

Ikan Bali
Balinese–style fish

Serves: 6

1 kg (2 lb 3 oz) fish steaks

peanut oil for frying

2 onions, finely chopped

2 garlic cloves, finely chopped

1½ teaspoons finely grated fresh ginger

1½ teaspoons Sambal ulek (page 104)

1 teaspoon finely grated lemon zest

1 teaspoon laos (dried galangal) powder or
  2 teaspoons grated fresh galangal

2 tablespoons lemon juice

2 tablespoons chopped dark palm sugar
  (jaggery)

2 tablespoons kecap manis

½ teaspoon salt

Wipe the fish with damp paper towel. Cut the fish into serving portions (see page 13).

Heat 2 tablespoons of the oil in a small saucepan over medium heat. Add the onion and cook until soft. Add the garlic and ginger and stir over medium heat until golden brown. Add the sambal ulek, lemon zest, laos powder, lemon juice, palm sugar, kecap manis and salt and simmer for 2–3 minutes. Remove from the heat and set aside.

Heat a little oil in a wok or large heavy-based saucepan over medium heat. When the oil is hot, fry the fish, in batches, until golden brown on both sides. Drain on paper towel. Serve with a little of the sauce spooned over the top.

Ikan Panggang (2)
Grilled fish with spices

Serves: 6

500 g (1 lb 2 oz) fish steaks, such as tuna

1 onion, roughly chopped

1 fresh red chilli, deseeded and chopped or ½ teaspoon Sambal ulek (page 104)

1 garlic clove

½ teaspoon dried shrimp paste

½ teaspoon kencur (aromatic ginger) powder

1 teaspoon salt

375 ml (12½ fl oz/1½ cups) thick coconut milk (pages 8–9)

1 stem lemongrass, bruised, or 2 strips lemon zest

2 tablespoons chopped fresh basil

lemon juice, to taste

vegetable oil for cooking

Wipe the fish with damp paper towel. Arrange the fish in a single layer in a glass dish.

Put the onion, chilli, garlic, shrimp paste, kencur powder and salt into a food processor with 125 ml (4 fl oz/½ cup) of the coconut milk and process until smooth. Alternatively, grate the onion and thinly slice the garlic and use sambal or chilli powder in place of fresh chilli, stirring to combine. Crush the shrimp paste and stir to combine with the coconut milk.

Marinate the fish in the spice mixture for about 1 hour, turning once.

Preheat the grill (broiler) until hot and line a tray with foil. Shake off and reserve the excess marinade and place the fish on the prepared tray. Put the marinade into a small saucepan with the remaining coconut milk, lemongrass and basil and simmer over low heat, stirring frequently to prevent curdling. Add the lemon juice and some salt, to taste.

Meanwhile, brush the fish with the oil and cook until the fish is golden, then turn the fish, brush with a little more oil and cook until golden and cooked through. If the fish steaks are large, divide into serving pieces. Arrange on a serving platter with the sauce spooned over the top.

Gulai Ikan
Fish in coconut milk and spices

Serves: 6

500 g (1 lb 2 oz) fish steaks, such as tuna, mackerel or kingfish

juice of ½ lemon

2 teaspoons tamarind pulp

2 onions, finely chopped

3 garlic cloves, crushed

2 teaspoons finely grated fresh ginger

1 teaspoon ground turmeric

½ teaspoon dried shrimp paste

1 teaspoon Sambal ulek (page 104) or chilli powder

1 stem lemongrass, bruised, or 2 strips lemon zest

1 teaspoon salt

375 ml (12½ fl oz/1½ cups) thin coconut milk (pages 8–9)

2 tablespoons chopped fresh basil

250 ml (8½ fl oz/1 cup) thick coconut milk (pages 8–9)

Wipe the fish with damp paper towel. Rub the fish with a little salt and the lemon juice and set aside.

Soak the tamarind pulp in 80 ml (2½ fl oz/⅓ cup) hot water for 10 minutes. Squeeze to dissolve the pulp in the water, then strain, discarding the seeds and fibre. Set aside.

Combine the onion, garlic, ginger, turmeric, shrimp paste, sambal ulek, lemongrass, salt and thin coconut milk in a saucepan. Bring to simmering point and simmer until the onion is soft and the liquid has thickened. Add the fish, basil and tamarind liquid and simmer until the fish is cooked through. Add the thick coconut milk and heat through but do not boil, stirring so that the coconut milk does not curdle. Serve with white rice, vegetables and sambals.

Fish and Seafood

Ikan Panggang Pedis
Grilled fish with chillies

Serves: 4–6

This very simple recipe was given to me by an Indonesian fish seller. If you like hot chillies as an accompaniment to fish, you will enjoy this dish. Buy the portion of fish just above the tail if possible, so that you avoid the stomach cavity.

1.5 kg (3 lb 5 oz) whole tuna or mackerel, cleaned and scaled

Sambal ulek (page 104) or fresh red chillies, ground

salt and lemon juice, to taste (optional)

Put the fish a good distance above glowing coals or place under a preheated grill (broiler). Cook slowly until the skin is very brown and the fish is cooked through.

Serve the fish, in portions, with sambal ulek or fresh chillies pounded to a pulp using a mortar and pestle. If you do not want too much heat in the sauce, remove the seeds first. Add a little salt and lemon juice to the chilli, if desired, and take tiny dabs with the fish.

Ikan Kacang
Fish with peanut sauce

Serves: 4–6

500 g (1 lb 2 oz) fish steaks

juice of 1 lemon

2 teaspoons tamarind pulp

2 tablespoons light soy sauce

2 tablespoons Peanut sauce (page 107)

125 ml (4 fl oz/½ cup) thick coconut milk (pages 8–9)

peanut oil for frying

1 tablespoon chopped fresh coriander (cilantro) leaves

Wipe the fish with damp paper towel. Rub the lemon juice over the fish and season generously with salt and freshly ground black pepper. Allow to stand for 15 minutes, then pat dry with paper towel.

Soak the tamarind pulp in 60 ml (2 fl oz/¼ cup) hot water for 10 minutes. Squeeze to dissolve the pulp in the water, then strain, discarding the seeds and fibre.

In a bowl, place 1 tablespoon of the tamarind liquid. Add the soy sauce, peanut sauce and coconut milk and stir to combine.

Heat the oil in a frying pan over medium heat. Add the fish and cook on both sides until golden. Pour off all but 1 tablespoon of the oil, add the peanut sauce mixture, spoon over the fish and cook until heated through. Sprinkle over the coriander, cover, and simmer for a further 5 minutes. Serve with rice.

Ikan Bandeng
Baked fish

Serves: 4–6

....

If you can get some large banana leaves to wrap the fish in, do so – they have a subtle and appetising aroma and look exotic when the dish is served at the table.

....

1.5 kg (3 lb 5 oz) whole snapper or jewfish, cleaned and scaled

2 teaspoons tamarind pulp

1 onion, chopped

2 garlic cloves

1 teaspoon finely chopped fresh ginger

1 tablespoon kecap manis

1 tablespoon peanut oil

1 teaspoon Sambal ulek (page 104) (optional)

1 teaspoon salt

1 teaspoon ground turmeric

2 squares banana leaf or foil for wrapping

3 tablespoons finely chopped fresh coriander (cilantro) leaves

Preheat the oven to 180°C (350°F). Wipe the fish with damp paper towel. Score the outside of the fish diagonally on each side.

Soak the tamarind pulp in 60 ml (2 fl oz/¼ cup) hot water for 10 minutes. Squeeze to dissolve the pulp in the water, then strain, discarding the seeds and fibre.

Put the onion, garlic, ginger, tamarind liquid, kecap manis, peanut oil, sambal ulek, if using, salt and turmeric into a food processor and process until smooth. Rub the spice mixture over the fish on both sides and put the remaining mixture inside the body cavity.

Arrange the banana leaves or foil in the base of a large baking dish and sit the fish on top. Sprinkle over the coriander leaves then fold the banana leaves over to enclose the fish. Secure with bamboo skewers.

Bake in the oven for 35–40 minutes, or until the fish is cooked through and the flesh flakes easily when tested with a fork. Transfer to a serving plate and open the banana leaves at the table.

Saté Udang
Skewered grilled prawns

Serves: 4

60 ml (2 fl oz/¼ cup) lemon juice

125 ml (4 fl oz/½ cup) thick coconut milk
(pages 8–9)

1 teaspoon Sambal ulek (page 104)

½ teaspoon dried shrimp paste

1 tablespoon kecap manis

1 teaspoon chopped dark palm sugar
(jaggery)

finely grated zest of 1 lemon

2 small garlic cloves, crushed with
1 teaspoon salt

750 g (1 lb 11 oz) raw prawns (shrimp),
peeled and deveined

vegetable oil

Soak bamboo skewers in cold water to prevent them from burning during cooking.

Put the lemon juice, coconut milk, sambal ulek, shrimp paste, kecap manis, palm sugar, lemon zest and garlic crushed with the salt into a bowl and stir well until the sugar has dissolved. Add the prawns, stir and marinate for 15 minutes or longer. If leaving for longer than 1 hour, cover and refrigerate. Drain the prawns, reserving the marinade.

Thread 3 or 4 prawns onto each skewer and brush lightly with the oil. Grill over hot coals or under a preheated grill (broiler) until they are lightly browned.

Meanwhile, put the reserved marinade into a saucepan over low heat. Simmer briefly, stirring constantly until heated through – you may need to add a little more coconut milk or soy sauce, to taste. Serve the sauce on the side of the prawns.

Ikan Bumbu Santan
Fried fish with spicy coconut milk

Serves: 4–6

....

2 × 500 g (1 lb 2 oz) whole oily fish, such as
  mullet or mackerel, cleaned and scaled,
  heads removed

oil for frying

2 onions, finely chopped

2 garlic cloves, crushed

1½ teaspoons finely grated fresh ginger

3–4 fresh red chillies, ground, or
  1 teaspoon Sambal ulek (page 104)

2 tablespoons salted soy beans (taucheo),
  drained and mashed (glossary)

1 teaspoon chopped dark palm sugar
  (jaggery)

250 ml (8½ fl oz/1 cup) coconut milk
  (pages 8–9)

a few sprigs fresh basil, to garnish

Butterfly the fish, lifting out the long bones that form the rib cage. Wipe the fish with paper towel dipped in coarse salt, cleaning away any black membrane.

Heat 2 tablespoons of the oil in a small saucepan over medium heat. Add the onion, garlic, ginger and chilli and cook over medium heat, stirring frequently, until the onion is soft and golden. Add the salted soy beans and cook for 2 minutes, then add the palm sugar and coconut milk and keep stirring while the mixture simmers and thickens. Keep warm.

Pour the oil into a large frying pan to a depth of 1 cm (½ in). When the oil is hot, cook one fish, skin side down, until brown, then turn and cook until cooked through. Drain on paper towel. Repeat with the other fish. Arrange both fish, skin side down, on a serving plate. Pour the warm sauce over, garnish with the basil and serve with rice.

Ikan Kecap
Fish in soy sauce

Serves: 4

500 g (1 lb 2 oz) fish steaks

2 teaspoons tamarind pulp

2 tablespoons peanut oil

1 onion, finely chopped

2–3 fresh red chillies, deseeded and chopped or 1 teaspoon Sambal ulek (page 104)

2 garlic cloves, finely chopped

1 teaspoon finely grated fresh ginger

½ teaspoon freshly ground black pepper

½ teaspoon kencur (aromatic ginger) powder

1 teaspoon laos (dried galangal) powder or 2 teaspoons grated fresh galangal

½ teaspoon freshly grated nutmeg

2 tablespoons kecap manis

2 teaspoons chopped dark palm sugar (jaggery)

Wipe the fish with damp paper towel. If large, cut the fish steaks into halves or quarters.

Soak the tamarind pulp in 60 ml (2 fl oz/¼ cup) hot water for 10 minutes. Squeeze to dissolve the pulp in the water, then strain, discarding the seeds and fibre.

Heat the peanut oil in a frying pan over low heat. Add the onion, chilli, garlic and ginger and cook for 5 minutes, or until the onion is soft and starts to colour, stirring occasionally. Add the pepper, kencur powder, laos powder and nutmeg and stir to combine.

Add the fish to the pan and cook for 2–3 minutes on each side, then add the tamarind liquid, kecap manis and palm sugar, cover, and simmer gently for 6–10 minutes, depending on the thickness of the fish, until just cooked through. Check after 5 minutes and if the liquid is drying up add 2 tablespoons hot water – the sauce should thicken but not cook away completely.

Serve the fish steaks with the sauce drizzled over the top and white rice, vegetable dishes and sambal to round off the meal.

Sambal Goreng Udang
Fried prawns with coconut milk

Serves: 4

....

500 g (1 lb 2 oz) raw prawns (shrimp), peeled and deveined (heads and shells reserved for stock)

60 ml (2 fl oz/¼ cup) peanut oil

6 daun salam leaves (glossary)

1 onion, finely chopped

2 fresh red chillies, deseeded and chopped

3 garlic cloves, finely chopped

1 teaspoon Sambal ulek (page 104)

½ teaspoon laos (dried galangal) powder or 1 teaspoon grated fresh galangal

125 ml (4 fl oz/½ cup) coconut cream (pages 8–9)

¾ teaspoon salt

½ teaspoon chopped dark palm sugar (jaggery)

To make the prawn stock, rinse the prawn heads and shells and drain well. Heat 1 tablespoon of the peanut oil in a saucepan and when very hot throw in the shells and heads. Stir-fry until they turn bright pink, then add 500 ml (17 fl oz/2 cups) hot water, bring to the boil, then reduce the heat to low and simmer until the liquid has reduced by half. Strain and reserve 125 ml (4 fl oz/½ cup) stock.

Heat the remaining oil in a frying pan over low heat. Add the daun salam leaves, onion, chilli and garlic, and cook for 5 minutes, or until the onion is soft and golden. Add the sambal ulek and laos powder and cook for a few seconds, then add the prawns and stir-fry until they change colour. Stir in the stock, coconut cream, salt and palm sugar and simmer until the liquid thickens and the oil starts to separate. Serve the fried prawns as an accompaniment to rice and curries.

Gulai Cumi-Cumi
Squid curry

Serves: 6

500 g (1 lb 2 oz) squid

1½ tablespoons tamarind pulp

1 onion, finely chopped

2 garlic cloves, crushed

1 teaspoon finely grated fresh ginger

1 teaspoon salt

1 teaspoon chilli powder

½ teaspoon dried shrimp paste

435 ml (15 fl oz/1¾ cups) coconut milk
(pages 8–9)

4 candlenuts or brazil nuts, grated

1 stem lemongrass, white part only, thinly
sliced, or 1 teaspoon finely grated lemon zest

1 teaspoon chopped dark palm sugar (jaggery)

Clean each squid, removing the ink sac and discarding the head. Rinse under cold running water and rub to remove the skin. Cut each squid tube into bite-sized pieces.

Soak the tamarind pulp in 80 ml (2½ fl oz/⅓ cup) hot water for 10 minutes. Squeeze to dissolve the pulp in the water, then strain, discarding the seeds and fibre.

Put the onion, garlic, ginger, salt, chilli powder, shrimp paste, coconut milk, candlenuts and lemongrass into a saucepan and bring to a simmer, stirring regularly. Allow to simmer until thickened. Add the squid and continue simmering for 5–6 minutes, then add the palm sugar and tamarind liquid, taste and add more salt if necessary. Serve hot with rice and vegetables.

Fish and Seafood

Sambal Cumi-Cumi Pedis
Squid fried with chillies

Serves: 6

250 g (9 oz) squid

4 large dried red chillies, chopped

2 teaspoons tamarind pulp

1 small onion, roughly chopped

3 garlic cloves

½ teaspoon dried shrimp paste

½ teaspoon salt

80 ml (2½ fl oz/⅓ cup) peanut oil

12 red bird's eye chillies, stalks removed

2 teaspoons chopped dark palm sugar
(jaggery)

Clean each squid, removing the ink sac and discarding the head. Rinse the tubes under cold running water and rub to remove the skin. Drain well and cut the tubes into rings.

Soak the chillies in hot water for 20 minutes. Drain and reserve the soaking liquid.

Soak the tamarind pulp in 60 ml (2 fl oz/¼ cup) hot water for 10 minutes. Squeeze to dissolve the pulp in the water, then strain, discarding the seeds and fibre.

Put the chillies into a food processor with the onion, garlic, shrimp paste and salt and process until smooth, adding a little of the liquid in which the chillies soaked if necessary.

Heat the oil in a heavy-based frying pan over medium heat. Add the chilli mixture and cook, stirring constantly, until the colour changes to a dark brownish red. Add the squid, tamarind liquid and bird's eye chillies and simmer, stirring occasionally, for 4–5 minutes. Stir in the palm sugar to combine. Serve hot with rice and curries.

Note

Bird's eye chillies are the hottest of hot! Unless you know what to expect, don't eat them. Do not crush them before cooking. Remember to warn your guests before they bite into a bird's eye chilli.

Poultry
and Eggs

❖

Opor Ayam
Chicken in coconut milk

Serves: 4–6

1.5 kg (3 lb 5 oz) chicken or chicken thighs
and drumsticks

3 garlic cloves, crushed

1 teaspoon salt, plus extra to taste

½ teaspoon freshly ground black pepper

1½ teaspoons finely grated fresh ginger

3 candlenuts or brazil nuts, finely grated

3 teaspoons ground coriander

1 teaspoon ground cumin

½ teaspoon ground fennel

½ teaspoon laos (dried galangal) powder or
2 teaspoons grated fresh galangal

80 ml (2½ fl oz/⅓ cup) oil

2 onions, thinly sliced

500 ml (17 fl oz/2 cups) thin coconut milk
(pages 8–9)

6 daun salam leaves (glossary)

1 stem lemongrass, or 3 strips thinly peeled
lemon zest

5 cm (2 in) cinnamon stick

375 ml (12½ fl oz/1½ cups) thick coconut
milk (pages 8–9)

1 tablespoon lemon juice

Fried onion flakes (page 105), to garnish

Joint the chicken (see page 13).

In a small bowl, combine the garlic, salt, pepper, ginger, candlenuts, coriander, cumin, fennel and laos powder. Stir to make a paste, adding a little of the oil if necessary. Rub the paste all over the chicken pieces to coat and leave to marinate for 1 hour.

Heat 2 tablespoons of the oil in a frying pan over low heat. Add the onion and cook until golden brown. Drain the oil and remove the onion to a plate.

Add the remaining oil to the pan over medium heat. Add the spiced chicken and cook until it just starts to colour. Add the thin coconut milk, daun salam leaves, lemongrass and cinnamon stick. Stir until it comes to the boil, then cook for 30 minutes, or until the chicken is tender. Add the thick coconut milk, stir thoroughly and cook for a further 15 minutes. Remove from the heat, add the lemon juice and season with salt, to taste. Remove the whole spices, garnish with the fried onions and serve the chicken with rice, vegetables and sambals.

Ayam Panggang
Roast spiced chicken

Serves: 4

Grilling over glowing coals is the best way to finish cooking this dish, but it can be roasted in the oven.

1.5 kg (3 lb 5 oz) whole chicken

2 tablespoons dark soy sauce

1 tablespoon lemon juice

1 onion, roughly chopped

2 garlic cloves

½ teaspoon Sambal ulek (page 104)

½ teaspoon freshly ground black pepper

½ teaspoon dried shrimp paste

125 ml (4 fl oz/½ cup) water or coconut milk

Preheat the oven to 190°C (375°F).

Cut the chicken in half lengthways, or split it open down the breast and open it out flat.

Put the soy sauce, lemon juice, onion and garlic into a food processor and process until smooth. Alternatively you can finely grate the onion and garlic and mix with the soy sauce and lemon juice.

Add the sambal ulek, pepper and shrimp paste to the onion mixture and rub all over the chicken. Leave to marinate for 30 minutes or longer.

Put the water or coconut milk into a large frying pan or wok over medium heat. Cook the chicken, skin side up, for 10 minutes, then turn, reduce the heat to low and cook for a further 10 minutes. Baste with the marinade and juices in the pan.

Transfer the chicken to a rack in a large roasting tin, skin side up, and pour in just enough water to come 1 cm (½ in) up the side of the tin. Spoon the marinade over the chicken and roast for 30 minutes, or until the skin is crisp and brown. Turn and cook the other side for 20–25 minutes. Alternatively you can finish cooking the chicken over hot coals – position the rack 10–15 cm (4–6 in) away from the heat so that the chicken can cook through before the skin gets too brown. Serve hot.

Singgang Ayam
Spiced grilled chicken

Serves: 6–8

In this recipe, the chicken is split down the breast and flattened, then marinated and simmered in coconut milk, and finally barbecued or cooked under the grill (broiler). If you do not have a pan large enough to accommodate a spread-eagled chicken, then cut the bird in half.

1.5 kg (3 lb 5 oz) whole chicken

1 large onion, roughly chopped

1 garlic clove

3 fresh red chillies, deseeded and chopped or 1½ teaspoons Sambal ulek (page 104)

2 teaspoons chopped fresh ginger

1 stem lemongrass, white part only, or 2 strips lemon zest

750 ml (25½ fl oz/3 cups) coconut milk (pages 8–9)

½ teaspoon ground turmeric

1 teaspoon freshly ground black pepper

2 teaspoons ground coriander

1½ teaspoons salt

4 dried daun salam leaves (glossary)

2 lime or lemon leaves

Split the chicken down the backbone and press down to flatten out the breastbone.

Put the onion, garlic, chilli, ginger and lemongrass into a food processor with 2–3 tablespoons of the coconut milk and process to a smooth paste. Add the turmeric, pepper, coriander and salt and a spoonful more coconut milk if necessary and process again for a few seconds. Spread some of this spice paste over the chicken and let it marinate for 30 minutes.

Put the remaining spice mixture in a wok or large heavy-based frying pan with the daun salam leaves, lime leaves and remaining coconut milk and bring to a simmer, stirring constantly. Add the chicken and continue simmering, basting the chicken occasionally. Turn after 10 minutes and simmer until cooked through. Transfer the chicken to a roasting tin and cook over hot coals or under a preheated grill (broiler), a good distance away from the heat source, until the chicken is brown.

Meanwhile, continue to simmer the sauce until it is thick. Serve a little sauce over the chicken and the rest on the side.

Ayam Goreng Jawa
Javanese–style fried chicken

Serves: 4–6

1.5 kg (3 lb 5 oz) whole chicken

1 onion, chopped

2 garlic cloves, crushed

1 teaspoon finely chopped fresh ginger

3 fresh red chillies, deseeded and chopped,
    or 1 teaspoon Sambal ulek (page 104)

2 candlenuts or brazil nuts

1 tablespoon desiccated (shredded) or
    grated fresh coconut

190 ml (6½ fl oz/¾ cup) coconut milk
    (pages 8–9)

2 teaspoons ground coriander

1 teaspoon laos (dried galangal) powder
    (optional)

½ teaspoon ground turmeric

1½ teaspoons salt

1 stem lemongrass or 3 strips lemon zest

6 dried daun salam leaves (glossary)

oil for deep-frying

Joint the chicken (see page 13). If large, cut the breast into quarters and wings into halves.

Put the onion, garlic, ginger, chilli, candlenuts, desiccated coconut and half of the coconut milk into a food processor and process until smooth.

Put the coconut mixture into a saucepan with the chicken pieces, remaining coconut milk, coriander, laos powder, if using, turmeric, salt, lemongrass and daun salam leaves. Bring to the boil, stirring, then reduce the heat to low and simmer until the chicken is tender and the sauce is thick and almost dry.

Meanwhile, heat the oil in a wok or large heavy-based saucepan over medium heat. When the oil is hot, deep-fry the chicken, turning to brown evenly on all sides. Serve the chicken pieces with white rice or Nasi goreng (page 21) and a sayur, or a curry with plenty of sauce.

Ayam Petis
Chicken with shrimp sauce

Serves: 6

1.5 kg (3 lb 5 oz) whole chicken

1 tablespoon peanut oil

1 large onion, finely chopped

4 garlic cloves, finely chopped

1 teaspoon finely grated fresh ginger

3 fresh red chillies, deseeded and chopped

1 teaspoon ground turmeric

1 teaspoon freshly ground black pepper

½ teaspoon dried shrimp paste

½ teaspoon laos (dried galangal) powder

1 stem lemongrass or 2 strips lemon zest

2 teaspoons shrimp sauce or 1 tablespoon fish sauce

1½ teaspoons salt

375 ml (12½ fl oz/1½ cups) coconut milk (pages 8–9)

1 tablespoon chopped dark palm sugar (jaggery)

2 tablespoons lemon juice

Joint the chicken (see page 13) and cut into serving pieces.

Heat the peanut oil in a large heavy-based frying pan over medium heat. Add the onion, garlic and ginger and cook until the onion is soft. Add the chilli, turmeric, pepper, shrimp paste and laos powder and stir-fry for 1 minute. Add the lemongrass, shrimp sauce, salt and chicken pieces and stir-fry over medium heat until the chicken is well coated.

Add the coconut milk and palm sugar to the pan and bring to simmering point, stirring frequently. Reduce the heat to low, and continue simmering for 30 minutes, or until the chicken is tender and the gravy has thickened. If the sauce is still not thick enough, remove the chicken pieces to a serving dish and reduce the sauce over high heat, stirring constantly. Add the lemon juice, pour the sauce over the chicken and serve with rice and sambals.

Poultry and Eggs

Ayam Goreng Asam
Piquant fried chicken

Serves: 6–8

1.5 kg (3 lb 5 oz) whole chicken
1 tablespoon tamarind pulp
3 garlic cloves, crushed, with 1½ teaspoons salt
1 teaspoon freshly ground black pepper
1 teaspoon chopped dark palm sugar (jaggery)
2 teaspoons ground coriander
1 teaspoon ground cumin
½ teaspoon ground turmeric
oil for frying

Joint the chicken (see page 13) and cut into serving pieces.

Soak the tamarind pulp in 80 ml (2½ fl oz/⅓ cup) hot water for 10 minutes. Squeeze to dissolve the pulp in the water, then strain, discarding the seeds and fibre.

In a bowl, combine the garlic with the pepper, palm sugar, coriander, cumin, turmeric and tamarind liquid. Rub over the chicken pieces and leave for 1 hour, or cover and marinate in the refrigerator overnight. Drain on paper towel to remove any excess moisture before cooking.

Pour the oil into a large frying pan to a depth of 1 cm (½ in). Cook the chicken over medium heat for 2 minutes on each side, turning regularly until golden brown. Reduce the heat, cover, and cook for 10–12 minutes further, turning the chicken after 5 minutes. Drain on paper towel and serve warm.

Ayam Bali
Balinese-style fried chicken

Serves: 4

1 onion, roughly chopped

2 garlic cloves

1 teaspoon chopped fresh ginger

3 fresh red chillies, deseeded and chopped

4 candlenuts or brazil nuts

1 tablespoon kecap manis

125 ml (4 fl oz/½ cup) peanut oil

1.25 kg (2 lb 12 oz) chicken wings and drumsticks

2 teaspoons chopped dark palm sugar (jaggery)

2 tablespoons lemon juice

½ teaspoon salt

250 ml (8½ fl oz/1 cup) coconut milk (pages 8–9)

Put the onion, garlic, ginger, chilli, candlenuts and kecap manis into a food processor and process to a smooth paste.

Heat the peanut oil in a wok or large heavy-based frying pan over high heat. Cook the chicken pieces until brown. Drain on paper towel.

Pour off all but 1 tablespoon of the oil from the pan and cook the chilli mixture for a few minutes, stirring constantly. Add the palm sugar, lemon juice, salt and coconut milk and bring to the boil, stirring often. Reduce the heat to low, return the chicken to the pan and simmer for 25 minutes, or until the chicken is tender and the sauce has thickened. Serve with rice or Fragrant rice (page 20), vegetables and other accompaniments

Ayam Panggang Pedis
Grilled chicken with hot spices

Serves: 6

1.5 kg (3 lb 5 oz) whole chicken

2 teaspoons salt

3 teaspoons freshly ground black pepper

3 teaspoons Sambal ulek (page 104) or ground fresh red chilli

2 tablespoons finely grated onion

2 garlic cloves, crushed

2 tablespoons dark soy sauce

2 teaspoons chopped dark palm sugar (jaggery)

2 tablespoons lemon juice

2 tablespoons peanut oil

Joint the chicken (see page 13) and cut into serving pieces. Use the tip of a sharp knife to score the skin and flesh to allow the flavours to penetrate.

Combine all the remaining ingredients in a bowl and rub over the chicken to coat. Leave to marinate for 1 hour or cover and refrigerate for longer.

Preheat a grill (broiler) to high or prepare a barbecue and have the coals glowing hot. Cook the chicken at a good distance from the heat so that it is cooked right through before the skin gets too brown. Brush with the marinade or some extra oil and keep turning the chicken until brown on all sides – test for doneness by piercing the thigh joint with a sharp knife; when cooked the juice should be clear, not pink.

Saté Ayam
Chicken grilled on skewers

Serves: 6

2 fresh red chillies, deseeded and chopped, or
½ teaspoon Sambal ulek (page 104)

2 onions, roughly chopped

1 teaspoon finely chopped fresh ginger

2 tablespoons lemon juice

1½ teaspoons salt

2 tablespoons light soy sauce

2 tablespoons dark soy sauce

2 tablespoons sesame oil, plus extra for brushing

2 tablespoons chopped dark palm sugar (jaggery)

750 g (1 lb 11 oz) boneless skinless chicken breasts
or thighs, cut into cubes

125 ml (4 fl oz/½ cup) thick coconut milk
(pages 8–9)

Soak 18 bamboo skewers in water to prevent them from burning during cooking.

Put the chilli, onion, ginger, lemon juice, salt and soy sauces in a food processor and process until smooth. Transfer to a bowl and stir in the sesame oil and palm sugar. Add the chicken and stir until each piece is well coated with the marinade. Leave to marinate for 1 hour or cover and refrigerate overnight.

Drain the chicken and reserve the marinade. Thread the chicken onto the skewers and grill over glowing coals or under a preheated grill (broiler), about 5 cm (2 in) from the heat, for 5–8 minutes, or until the chicken is crisp and brown. Turn and brush with extra oil while cooking.

Put the reserved marinade into a small saucepan, add the thick coconut milk and simmer over low heat until smooth and thickened, stirring constantly. Pour into a small bowl and serve with the satay skewers.

Sambal Goreng Telur
Eggs in chilli sauce

Serves: 6

....

This is a very hot dish, intended as a sambal or accompaniment, and therefore half a hard-boiled egg per serving is sufficient.

....

60 ml (2 fl oz/¼ cup) peanut oil

1 onion, finely chopped

1 garlic clove, crushed

½ teaspoon dried shrimp paste

3 teaspoons Sambal ulek (page 104) or chilli powder

½ teaspoon laos (dried galangal) powder or
   1 teaspoon grated fresh galangal

3 candlenuts or brazil nuts, finely grated

½ teaspoon salt

2 teaspoons chopped dark palm sugar (jaggery)

125 ml (4 fl oz/½ cup) coconut milk (pages 8–9)

lemon juice, to taste

3 hard-boiled eggs, peeled and halved

Heat the oil in a wok or large heavy-based saucepan and cook the onion and garlic until the onion is soft and golden. Add the shrimp paste, sambal ulek, laos powder and candlenuts and cook for a few seconds, crushing the shrimp paste with a spoon. Add the salt, palm sugar, coconut milk and lemon juice and simmer gently, stirring constantly, until thick and oily in appearance.

Add the egg halves, spooning the sauce over them. Serve hot or at room temperature.

Pindaing Telur
Eggs in soy sauce

Serves: 4–6

....

2 tablespoons peanut oil

1 small onion, thinly sliced

1 fresh red chilli, deseeded and sliced

1 garlic clove, crushed

½ teaspoon finely grated fresh ginger

½ teaspoon dried shrimp paste

1 large ripe tomato, diced

1 tablespoon vinegar

½ teaspoon salt

1 tablespoon chopped dark palm sugar (jaggery)

60 ml (2 fl oz/¼ cup) light soy sauce

4–6 hard-boiled eggs, peeled and halved

Heat the peanut oil in a saucepan over low heat. Add the onion, chilli, garlic and ginger and cook until the onion is soft and starts to turn golden. Add the shrimp paste and cook, mashing with the back of a spoon. Add the tomato and cook, stirring, until the tomato has turned into a pulp. Add the vinegar, salt, palm sugar, soy sauce and 125 ml (4 fl oz/½ cup) water, cover, and simmer until the sauce has thickened. Add the egg halves and continue to simmer until the egg has just heated through. Serve immediately.

Tahu Telur
Tofu omelettes

Serves: 4

150 g (5½ oz) fresh firm or soft tofu, diced or mashed

3 eggs, beaten

6 spring onions (scallions), thinly sliced, plus extra to garnish

½ teaspoon salt

¼ teaspoon freshly ground black pepper

peanut oil for frying

Sauce

1 tablespoon oil

1 small onion, very finely chopped

2 garlic cloves, finely chopped

1 firm ripe tomato, finely chopped

2 tablespoons kecap manis

1 tablespoon sugar

To make the sauce, heat the oil in a small saucepan over low heat. Add the onion and garlic and cook for about 5 minutes, stirring often, until the onion is soft. Add the tomato and cook for 3–4 minutes, stirring until the tomato is cooked to a pulp. Add the kecap manis, sugar and 2 tablespoons water and bring to the boil briefly. This sauce can be made ahead of time and reheated before serving.

To make the omelettes, stir together the tofu, egg and spring onion in a bowl and season with the salt and pepper. Heat a little oil in a large heavy-based frying pan over low heat and pour in one-quarter of the egg mixture to make a small round omelette no larger than saucer size. Repeat to make another 3 omelettes and keep warm. To serve, pour some of the warm sauce over each omelette and garnish with the spring onion.

Meat

❖

Daging Masak Bali
Balinese–style beef strips

Serves: 6

2 teaspoons tamarind pulp

1 onion, roughly chopped

3 garlic cloves

1 tablespoon chopped fresh ginger

4–6 fresh red chillies, deseeded and chopped

½ teaspoon dried shrimp paste

60 ml (2 fl oz/¼ cup) peanut oil

750 g (1 lb 11 oz) blade steak, thinly sliced
   into strips

2 tablespoons dark soy sauce

2 teaspoons chopped dark palm sugar (jaggery)

Soak the tamarind pulp in 60 ml (2 fl oz/¼ cup) hot water for 10 minutes. Squeeze to dissolve the pulp in the water, then strain, discarding the seeds and fibre. Measure 2 tablespoons of the liquid and set aside.

Put the onion, garlic, ginger, chilli and shrimp paste in a food processor and process until smooth.

Heat the peanut oil in a wok or large heavy-based frying pan and cook the chilli mixture for about 5 minutes, stirring constantly, until it no longer sticks to the pan and the oil starts to separate. Add the beef and continue to stir-fry until it changes colour.

Add the tamarind liquid, soy sauce and 250 ml (8½ fl oz/ 1 cup) water to the wok, cover, and simmer gently until the beef is tender. Uncover and cook until the liquid has almost evaporated. Stir in the palm sugar and season with salt, to taste. Serve with boiled rice, vegetables and sambals.

Lapis Daging Semarang
Semarang–style sliced beef

Serves: 4

500 g (1 lb 2 oz) thinly sliced lean topside, rump
   or round steaks

1 onion, roughly chopped

4 garlic cloves

1 teaspoon freshly ground black pepper

60 ml (2 fl oz/¼ cup) kecap manis

2 tablespoons chopped dark palm sugar (jaggery)

2 tablespoons peanut oil

2 ripe tomatoes, chopped

Beat out the steaks thinly using a meat mallet, taking care not to break through the slices.

Put the onion, garlic, pepper, kecap manis and palm sugar into a food processor and process until smooth. Transfer the onion mixture to a dish, add the steaks and leave to marinate for 1 hour or cover and refrigerate for longer. Drain the steaks, reserving the marinade.

Heat the peanut oil in a wok or large heavy-based frying pan over high heat. Cook the steaks on both sides until brown. Add the reserved marinade and tomato and cook over medium heat for about 12 minutes, stirring frequently, until the sauce has thickened and the meat is tender. Serve immediately.

Singgang Daging
Beef spareribs special

Serves: 4–6

1.5 kg (3 lb 5 oz) beef spareribs, cut into short lengths

3 garlic cloves, crushed

1 teaspoon finely grated fresh ginger

1 teaspoon salt

60 ml (2 fl oz/¼ cup) peanut oil

60 ml (2 fl oz/¼ cup) kecap manis

2 tablespoons dry sherry

½ teaspoon Chinese five-spice

¼ teaspoon freshly ground black pepper

1 tablespoon chopped dark palm sugar (jaggery) or honey

Rub the spareribs with the combined garlic, ginger and salt. Put all the remaining ingredients, except the palm sugar, into a bowl. Add 125 ml (4 fl oz/½ cup) water and stir to combine.

Heat the oil in a wok or large heavy-based frying pan over high heat. Cook the beef for 5–6 minutes, or until the ribs are browned. Pour the sauce over the ribs, bring to the boil, then reduce the heat to low, cover, and simmer until the meat on the ribs is very tender and the sauce has reduced. Uncover, stir in the palm sugar until it has dissolved, then serve hot.

The ribs can be roasted in a preheated 180°C (350°F) oven for a few minutes until further glazed and browned, if desired.

Abon Daging
Shredded crisp-fried meat

Makes: 3 cups

This will be a curious preparation to those not familiar with Asian foods, but it is typical of the strongly flavoured dishes referred to colloquially as 'rice pullers'. The chief ingredient might be fish, prawns or, as in this case, red meat. Thoroughly cooked and then fried until crisp, it can be bottled and kept for weeks to sprinkle over rice and make a meal more appetising. The first time I made abon daging I had spent the better part of an hour shredding the meat with a mallet, and then I realised it would have been much easier putting small amounts, about 2 tablespoons at a time, into a food processor. If processed for longer than 4–5 seconds at a time, the meat will turn into a paste, so be careful.

750 g (1 lb 11 oz) lean topside or round steak

2 teaspoons salt

1 tablespoon tamarind pulp

3 garlic cloves, crushed with ½ teaspoon salt

1 teaspoon shrimp sauce or 1 tablespoon fish sauce

½ teaspoon freshly ground black pepper

1 teaspoon chilli powder (optional)

2 teaspoons ground coriander

1 teaspoon ground cumin

125 ml (4 fl oz/½ cup) peanut oil

4 dried red chillies

4 tablespoons dried onion flakes

2 teaspoons dried garlic granules

Put the steak into a large saucepan with enough water to cover, add the salt and bring to the boil. Reduce the heat to low, cover, and simmer for 1½–2 hours, or until the meat is so tender it will pull apart with a spoon. Remove from the cooking liquid (you can save it to use in a soup) and drain in a colander until dry and cool. Break up the meat into small pieces and use a meat mallet to pound it to very fine shreds or use a food processor as described above.

Soak the tamarind pulp in 125 ml (4 fl oz/½ cup) hot water for 10 minutes. Squeeze to dissolve the pulp in the water, then strain, discarding the seeds and fibre. Add the garlic, shrimp sauce, pepper, chilli powder, coriander and cumin. Add the meat and toss to coat.

Heat the peanut oil in a wok or large heavy-based frying pan over low heat. Cook the whole dried chillies for a few seconds, then drain on paper towel, cool, then remove the stems and seeds and finely chop. Put the onion flakes in a wire strainer and lower into the oil for a few seconds, just until they turn golden. Drain on paper towel. In the same wire strainer fry the dried garlic for 2–3 seconds. Drain on paper towel and set aside to cool.

Add the meat to the oil in the wok and stir-fry for about 3–4 minutes, or until it is a rich brown. Drain and cool on paper towel. When the meat is quite cold sprinkle with a little extra salt, to taste, and toss through the chilli, onion and dried garlic. If liked, a teaspoon of sugar can be mixed in. Store in an airtight container for up to 1 month.

Dendeng Ragi
Dry-fried meat and coconut

Serves: 6

1 tablespoon tamarind pulp

90 g (3 oz/1 cup) desiccated (shredded) coconut

1 onion, grated

2 garlic cloves, crushed

1½ teaspoons salt

1 teaspoon freshly ground black pepper

3 teaspoons ground coriander

1 teaspoon ground cumin

1 teaspoon Sambal ulek (page 104) or 2 fresh red chillies, finely chopped

2 teaspoons chopped dark palm sugar (jaggery)

500 g (1 lb 2 oz) topside or round steak, thinly sliced into strips

80 ml (2½ fl oz/⅓ cup) peanut oil

Soak the tamarind pulp in 125 ml (4 fl oz/½ cup) hot water for 10 minutes. Squeeze to dissolve the pulp in the water, then strain, discarding the seeds and fibre. Add all the remaining ingredients, except the steak and peanut oil, to the tamarind liquid. Add 60 ml (2 fl oz/¼ cup) water and stir well to combine. Add the steak and toss to coat.

Put the meat and coconut mixture into a large heavy-based saucepan over low heat. Cover and cook until the meat changes colour. Uncover and continue to cook and stir the meat until all the liquid has been absorbed and the meat is quite dry – take care that the coconut does not stick to the pan.

Heat the peanut oil in a wok or large heavy-based frying pan. Transfer the beef to the wok and stir-fry until dark brown and crisp. Serve as an accompaniment with rice and vegetable dishes.

Rendang Ginjal
Dry-fried kidney curry

Serves: 6

750 g (1 lb 11 oz) ox kidney, core removed and meat diced

1 teaspoon finely grated fresh ginger

2 garlic cloves, crushed with 1 teaspoon salt

2 teaspoons tamarind pulp

60 ml (2 fl oz/¼ cup) peanut oil

2 onions, finely chopped

1 teaspoon ground turmeric

2 teaspoons ground coriander

1 teaspoon ground cumin

½ teaspoon ground fennel

½ teaspoon freshly ground black pepper

1 teaspoon chilli powder or 2 fresh red chillies, deseeded and chopped

3 candlenuts or brazil nuts, finely grated

500 ml (17 fl oz/2 cups) coconut milk (pages 8–9)

1 small cinnamon stick

2 teaspoons chopped dark palm sugar (jaggery)

Rub the kidneys with the ginger and garlic and set aside. Soak the tamarind pulp in 60 ml (2 fl oz/¼ cup) hot water for 10 minutes. Squeeze to dissolve the pulp in the water, then strain, discarding the seeds and fibre. Measure 2 tablespoons of the liquid and set aside.

Heat the oil in a wok or large heavy-based frying pan over medium heat. Add the onion and cook until it is soft and golden. Add the turmeric, coriander, cumin, fennel and pepper and stir-fry for 1 minute, then add the chilli powder, candlenuts and kidneys, and continue to cook until the kidneys change colour. Add the coconut milk and cinnamon stick and simmer gently for 2 hours, stirring occasionally, until the sauce has reduced and thickened. As the mixture thickens it will be necessary to stir more frequently. Add the tamarind liquid and palm sugar, stir well to combine, and cook for a few minutes longer. Serve hot.

Rendang Daging
Dry-fried beef curry

Serves: 8

It is worth making a large quantity of this because it keeps so well, developing more flavour each day.

1 tablespoon tamarind pulp

2 onions, roughly chopped

6 garlic cloves

1 tablespoon finely chopped fresh ginger

6 fresh red chillies, deseeded and chopped

500 ml (17 fl oz/2 cups) thick coconut milk
  (pages 8–9)

1½ teaspoons salt

1 teaspoon ground turmeric

1 teaspoon chilli powder (optional)

2 teaspoons ground coriander

6 dried daun salam leaves (glossary)

1 stem lemongrass or 1 strip lemon zest

1 teaspoon grated fresh galangal

1.5 kg (3 lb 5 oz) chuck, blade or round
  steak, thinly sliced into strips

2 teaspoons sugar

Soak the tamarind pulp in 125 ml (4 fl oz/½ cup) hot water for 10 minutes. Squeeze to dissolve the pulp in the water, then strain, discarding the seeds and fibre. Set aside.

Put the onion, garlic, ginger, chilli and 125 ml (4 fl oz/½ cup) of the coconut milk in a food processor and process until smooth. Pour into a large saucepan and add the remaining coconut milk. Add the salt, turmeric, chilli powder, if using, coriander, daun salam leaves, lemongrass and galangal and stir to combine. Add the meat and bring to the boil.

Reduce the heat to medium, add the tamarind liquid and simmer until the sauce has thickened, stirring occasionally. Reduce the heat to low and continue simmering for about 2½ hours, or until the sauce is almost dry, stirring frequently to ensure the mixture does not stick to the pan. When the oil starts to separate, add the sugar and stir to dissolve – allow the meat to cook in the oil until it is dark brown. Serve with white rice, one or two vegetable dishes, sambals and Prawn crisps (page 31).

Semur Daging
Beef cooked in soy sauce

Serves: 4–6

Spicy, sweet and salty all at the same time, this simple recipe will be a favourite with children as well as adults.

2 teaspoons tamarind pulp

2 tablespoons peanut oil

1 large onion, finely chopped

2 garlic cloves, crushed with ½ teaspoon salt

1 teaspoon finely grated fresh ginger

500 g (1 lb 2 oz) chuck or round steak, cut into 3 cm (1¼ in) cubes

½ teaspoon freshly ground black pepper

¼ teaspoon ground cardamom

¼ teaspoon ground cinnamon

¼ teaspoon freshly grated nutmeg

⅛ teaspoon ground cloves

60 ml (2 fl oz/¼ cup) kecap manis

1 tablespoon chopped dark palm sugar (jaggery)

Soak the tamarind pulp in 60 ml (2 fl oz/¼ cup) hot water for 10 minutes. Squeeze to dissolve the pulp in the water, then strain, discarding the seeds and fibre. Measure 2 tablespoons of the liquid and set aside.

Heat the peanut oil in a wok or large heavy-based frying pan over low heat. Add the onion and cook until it is soft. Add the garlic and ginger and stir-fry until the onion starts to colour. Add the meat and stir-fry until it changes colour. Add the ground spices, kecap manis, palm sugar, tamarind liquid and 250 ml (8½ fl oz/1 cup) water. Bring to the boil, then reduce the heat to low, cover, and simmer for 1¼ hours, or until the meat is tender and the sauce has reduced. Serve with white rice and vegetables.

Rendang
Dry meat curry

Serves: 8

....

2 garlic cloves

1 tablespoon finely grated fresh ginger

2 onions, thinly sliced

1 kg (2 lb 3 oz) beef or mutton, cut into
large cubes

2 teaspoons tamarind pulp

60 ml (2 fl oz/¼ cup) peanut oil

1 small cinnamon stick

4–5 whole cloves

3 teaspoons ground coriander

1 teaspoon ground cumin

1 teaspoon freshly ground black pepper

1 teaspoon chilli powder, or to taste

½ teaspoon ground fennel

½ teaspoon ground kencur (aromatic
ginger) powder

1 tablespoon desiccated (shredded)
coconut, toasted

1 litre (34 fl oz/4 cups) thin coconut milk
(pages 8–9)

2 teaspoons salt

250 ml (8½ fl oz/1 cup) thick coconut milk
(pages 8–9)

Put the garlic, ginger and half of the onion into a
food processor and process to a smooth purée, adding
2 tablespoons of thin coconut milk if needed. Transfer
to a bowl, add the meat and toss to coat. Set aside.

Soak the tamarind pulp in 60 ml (2 fl oz/¼ cup) hot water
for 10 minutes. Squeeze to dissolve the pulp in the water,
then strain, discarding the seeds and fibre. Set aside.

Heat the peanut oil in a large heavy-based saucepan over
medium heat. Add the remaining onion, cinnamon stick
and whole cloves, stirring occasionally, until the onion is soft
and starts to turn golden. Add the meat and stir-fry until
the meat changes colour. Add the ground spices, desiccated
coconut, thin coconut milk and salt. Bring to the boil,
stirring constantly, and boil for 10 minutes, then reduce
the heat to low and simmer until the meat is almost tender.
Add the tamarind liquid, stir well and simmer until the
liquid has evaporated. Add the thick coconut milk, stirring
constantly, and allow to simmer again until the oil starts to
separate and the curry is very dry.

Empal Jawa
Beef in soy sauce and chillies

Serves: 6

500 g (1 lb 2 oz) topside, round or
   rump steak

60 ml (2 fl oz/¼ cup) peanut oil

1 onion, finely chopped

3 garlic cloves, crushed

1½ teaspoons Sambal ulek (page 104) or
   2 fresh red chillies, deseeded and finely
   chopped

½ teaspoon dried shrimp paste

¾ teaspoon laos (dried galangal) powder or
   1 teaspoon grated fresh galangal

2 teaspoons finely grated lemongrass or
   1 teaspoon finely chopped lemon zest

2 tablespoons kecap manis

1 teaspoon chopped dark palm sugar
   (jaggery)

Put the meat into a saucepan with just enough water to cover. Bring to the boil, then reduce the heat to low and simmer for 15 minutes. Allow the meat to cool to lukewarm in the broth. When cool enough to handle, slice the meat into thin strips, reserving 60 ml (2 fl oz/¼ cup) of the broth.

Heat the peanut oil in a wok or large heavy-based frying pan over low heat. Add the onion and cook until soft. Add the garlic, sambal ulek, shrimp paste, laos powder and lemongrass and cook until the onion turns golden, crushing the shrimp paste with the back of a spoon.

Increase the heat to medium, add the beef to the pan and stir-fry for 3–4 minutes. Add the kecap manis, palm sugar and reserved broth, reduce the heat to low and simmer until the liquid has almost evaporated and the oil starts to separate. Serve hot with rice and vegetable dishes.

Dendeng
Dried spiced meat

Serves: 12

Prepared this way, meat can be kept for a long while without spoiling. Use raw meat or remember this recipe when you've roasted a big piece of meat and it has been disappointing and tough – this is a good way to use up the leftovers. Serve as an accompaniment to a meal of rice, vegetables and sambal.

2 teaspoons tamarind pulp

100 ml (3½ fl oz) peanut oil

2 garlic cloves, crushed

½ teaspoon finely grated fresh ginger

2 teaspoons ground coriander

1 teaspoon ground cumin

1 teaspoon shrimp sauce or ½ teaspoon dried shrimp paste

1½ teaspoons salt

1 teaspoon Sambal ulek (page 104)

125 ml (4 fl oz/½ cup) kecap manis

1 kg (2 lb 3 oz) round or topside steak, thinly sliced into strips

3 teaspoons chopped dark palm sugar (jaggery)

Preheat the oven to 120°C (250°F). Soak the tamarind pulp in 60 ml (2 fl oz/¼ cup) hot water for 10 minutes. Squeeze to dissolve the pulp in the water, then strain, discarding the seeds and fibre. Measure 2 tablespoons of the liquid and set aside.

Heat the peanut oil in a wok or large heavy-based frying pan over medium heat. Add the garlic, ginger, coriander, cumin and shrimp sauce and stir-fry for 1–2 minutes, then add the salt, sambal ulek, kecap manis and tamarind liquid. Add the meat and stir to coat. Reduce the heat to low, cover, and cook for 30–35 minutes, stirring often, until the liquid has almost evaporated. Add the palm sugar and stir well to dissolve.

Remove the pan from the heat and spread the meat in a baking dish in a single layer. Continue cooking in the oven for 30 minutes, then turn the meat and cook for a further 20–30 minutes, or until the meat is dark brown but not burnt, and the oil is visible at the edge of the pan. Cool and store in an airtight container for up to 1 month.

Asam Babi Goreng
Fried tamarind pork (Bali)

Serves: 4–6

1 tablespoon tamarind pulp

1 onion, roughly chopped

2 garlic cloves

2 teaspoons finely grated fresh ginger

2 tablespoons kecap manis

1 teaspoon Sambal ulek (page 104) or
    2 fresh red chillies, deseeded and chopped

1 tablespoon oil

500 g (1 lb 2 oz) pork spareribs, cut into
    short lengths

½ teaspoon salt

2 teaspoons chopped dark palm sugar
    (jaggery)

Soak the tamarind pulp in 80 ml (2½ fl oz/⅓ cup) hot water for 10 minutes. Squeeze to dissolve the pulp in the water, then strain, discarding the seeds and fibre. Set aside.

Put the onion, garlic, ginger, kecap manis and sambal ulek into a food processor and process until smooth.

Heat the oil in a wok or large heavy-based frying pan over high heat. Add the pork and cook, turning often, until brown all over. Reduce the heat to medium, pour off any excess fat, then add the onion mixture and stir-fry for 5 minutes. Add the tamarind liquid, salt and 60 ml (2 fl oz/¼ cup) hot water. Reduce the heat to low, cover and simmer 25–30 minutes. Add the palm sugar and cook uncovered, stirring regularly, until the sauce is dark and almost dry. Serve hot.

Saté Babi

Pork satay

Serves: 6

---

1 onion, roughly chopped

1 garlic clove

1 teaspoon finely grated fresh ginger

1 tablespoon lemon juice

2 tablespoons kecap manis

1 teaspoon Sambal ulek (page 104) or
    2 fresh red chillies, deseeded and chopped

½ teaspoon salt

1 teaspoon chopped dark palm sugar
    (jaggery)

2 tablespoons peanut oil

1 kg (2 lb 3 oz) pork fillet or boned pork loin,
    trimmed and cut into 2 cm (¾ in) cubes

Soak 18 bamboo skewers in cold water to prevent them from burning during cooking.

Put the onion, garlic, ginger, lemon juice, kecap manis, sambal ulek, salt and palm sugar into a food processor and process until smooth. Pour into a bowl, stir in the peanut oil, then add the pork and toss to coat. Leave to marinate for at least 1 hour or cover and refrigerate for longer.

Thread 5 or 6 pork cubes onto each skewer. Grill the skewers over hot coals or under a preheated grill (broiler) for 6–7 minutes on each side, or until the pork is brown on all sides. Do not put too close to the heat or the outside will brown before the pork is cooked through. Serve hot.

Pergedel Goreng Jawa
Javanese-style fried meatballs

Makes: about 60–70 meatballs

Freely adopted from Dutch frikkadels, with hot chillies and spices giving a local flavour, these meatballs can be served hot as a snack or cold as picnic fare.

500 g (1 lb 2 oz) minced (ground) beef

2 onions, finely chopped

2 garlic cloves, crushed with 1 teaspoon salt

2 fresh red chillies, deseeded and finely chopped or 1 teaspoon Sambal ulek (page 104)

500 g (1 lb 2 oz) floury potatoes, boiled and mashed

2 teaspoons chopped dark palm sugar (jaggery)

½ teaspoon dried shrimp paste

1 tablespoon dark soy sauce

1 tablespoon lemon juice

3 teaspoons ground coriander

2 teaspoons ground cumin

1 teaspoon freshly grated nutmeg or ground mace

1 egg, beaten

peanut oil for deep-frying

Put the beef into a large bowl. Add the onion, garlic, chilli and mashed potato and use your hands to combine.

In a small bowl, dissolve the palm sugar and shrimp paste in the combined soy sauce and lemon juice, then stir in the coriander, cumin and nutmeg. Add to the minced meat with the egg and continue to mix all the ingredients together until well combined. Take small portions of the mixture at a time and shape into small balls. Cover and refrigerate for at least 1 hour.

Heat the peanut oil in a wok or large heavy-based saucepan over medium heat. When the oil is hot, deep-fry the balls, in batches, for 3–4 minutes, turning regularly, until brown on all sides and cooked through. Drain on paper towel and serve.

Rempah-Rempah
Meat and coconut patties

Makes: 30 flat patties or 60 small balls

245 g (8½ oz/2¾ cups) desiccated
  (shredded) coconut

500 g (1 lb 2 oz) minced (ground) beef

½ teaspoon dried shrimp paste

2 garlic cloves, crushed with 1½ teaspoons salt

½ teaspoon freshly ground black pepper

1½ teaspoons ground coriander

1 teaspoon ground cumin

½ teaspoon kencur (aromatic ginger) powder

2 eggs, beaten

peanut oil for deep-frying

Put the coconut into a bowl with 125 ml (4 fl oz/½ cup) hot water and mix well until the coconut is moistened. Put into a large bowl with the beef.

Put the shrimp paste in a bowl and crush with the back of a spoon, then dissolve in 1 tablespoon hot water. Add the garlic, pepper, coriander, cumin, kencur powder and egg and mix well to combine. Pour over the meat and use your hands to mix all the ingredients together until well combined. Shape into small patties or balls. Cover and refrigerate for at least 1 hour.

Heat the peanut oil in a wok or large heavy-based saucepan over medium heat. When the oil is hot, deep-fry the balls, in batches, for 3–4 minutes, turning regularly, until brown on all sides and cooked through. Drain on paper towel and serve as an accompaniment to a rice dish or as a snack by themselves. Serve cold at picnics. The balls, if made small enough, are ideal to serve with drinks.

Saté Kambing Madura
Madurese-style lamb satay

Serves: 4–6

1 teaspoon tamarind pulp

1 small onion, grated

2 garlic cloves, crushed with ½ teaspoon salt

1 teaspoon Sambal ulek (page 104) or
  2 fresh red chillies, deseeded and chopped

½ teaspoon dried shrimp paste

1 tablespoon kecap manis

2 tablespoons freshly grated coconut or use
  desiccated (shredded) coconut moistened
  with 1 tablespoon hot water

500 g (1 lb 2 oz) boneless leg of lamb,
  cut into small cubes

Soak 18 bamboo skewers in cold water to prevent them from burning during cooking.

Soak the tamarind pulp in 1 tablespoon hot water for 10 minutes. Squeeze to dissolve the pulp in the water, then strain, discarding the seeds and fibre. Add the onion, garlic, sambal ulek, shrimp paste, kecap manis and coconut, stirring well to combine. Add the lamb and toss to coat. Leave to marinate for 2 hours or cover and refrigerate for longer.

Thread some of the lamb onto each skewer. Grill the skewers over hot coals or under a preheated grill (broiler) for 6–7 minutes on each side, or until the lamb is cooked through and brown on all sides. Serve with rice and satay sauce (opposite).

Saté Manis
Sweet satay

Serves: 4–6

1 tablespoon chopped dark palm sugar (jaggery)

3 garlic cloves, crushed

½ teaspoon salt

2 tablespoons kecap manis

1 tablespoon oil

2 teaspoons ground cumin

750 g (1 lb 11 oz) rump steak or pork fillet, cut into 2 cm (¾ in) cubes

Satay sauce

1 tablespoon tamarind pulp

125 ml (4 fl oz/½ cup) peanut sauce (page 107)

2 teaspoons Sambal bajak (page 112)

Soak 18 bamboo skewers in cold water to prevent them from burning during cooking.

In a large shallow baking dish, combine the palm sugar, garlic, salt, kecap manis, oil and cumin and stir until the sugar has dissolved. Thread 4–5 pieces of meat onto each skewer and arrange the skewers in the marinade, turning to coat. Leave to marinate for 2 hours or cover and refrigerate for longer.

Meanwhile, make the satay sauce. Soak the tamarind pulp in 60 ml (2 fl oz/¼ cup) hot water for 10 minutes. Squeeze to dissolve the pulp in the water, then strain, discarding the seeds and fibre.

In a bowl, combine 2 tablespoons of the tamarind liquid with the peanut sauce, sambal bajak and 60 ml (2 fl oz/¼ cup) water and stir to combine. Set aside until ready to serve.

Grill the skewers over hot coals or under a preheated grill (broiler) for 6–7 minutes on each side, or until the meat is cooked through and brown on all sides. Serve hot with the satay sauce on the side.

Saté Bumbu
Spicy beef satay

Serves: 4–5

Unlike most other satays with their small cubes of meat, this one features a long, thin, finely sliced strip of meat which is threaded on the skewers like a ruffled ribbon. After being briefly stir-fried in a marinade it is then cooked over coals or under a grill (broiler).

2 teaspoons tamarind pulp

2 tablespoons kecap manis

1 onion, roughly chopped

2 garlic cloves

½ teaspoon laos (dried galangal) powder (optional)

½ teaspoon Sambal ulek (page 104)

½ teaspoon freshly ground black pepper

½ teaspoon dried shrimp paste

2 tablespoons peanut oil

500 g (1 lb 2 oz) topside, round or blade steak, thinly sliced into strips

125 ml (4 fl oz/½ cup) coconut milk (pages 8–9)

6 dried daun salam leaves (glossary)

1 stem lemongrass or 2 strips lemon zest

2 teaspoons chopped dark palm sugar (jaggery)

Soak 18 bamboo skewers in cold water to prevent them from burning during cooking.

Soak the tamarind pulp in 60 ml (2 fl oz/¼ cup) hot water for 10 minutes. Squeeze to dissolve the pulp in the water, then strain, discarding the seeds and fibre. Measure 2 tablespoons of the liquid and set aside.

Place the tamarind liquid into a food processor with the kecap manis, onion and garlic and process to make a smooth paste. Stir in the laos powder, if using, sambal ulek, pepper and shrimp paste, using the back of a spoon to crush the paste.

Heat the peanut oil in a wok or large heavy-based frying pan over medium heat. Add the spice paste and stir-fry until it turns brown and comes away from the side of the wok.

Add the meat to the wok and stir-fry for about 1 minute, or until the meat changes colour. Add the coconut milk, daun salam leaves, lemongrass and palm sugar, stirring to combine. Reduce the heat and simmer until the sauce is very thick and almost dry. Remove from the heat and allow to cool slightly, then thread the beef strips onto the skewers.

Grill the skewers over hot coals or under a preheated grill (broiler) for 6–7 minutes on each side, or until the beef is cooked through and brown on all sides. If there is any leftover sauce in the wok, spoon it over the meat skewers to serve.

Vegetables

Gulai Manis Kangkung
Watercress in sweet gravy

Serves: 6

Kangkung is a dark green leaf vegetable used in Asian countries and is highly prized for its vitamin value. Substitute watercress, English spinach or witlof (Belgian endive/chicory). Although witlof is bitter, this preparation contains sugar, and the resulting bitter–sweet combination is fascinating.

500 g (1 lb 2 oz) kangkung, or English spinach or chicory

35 g (¾ cup) dried shrimp

375 ml (12½ fl oz/1½ cups) thin coconut milk (pages 8–9)

1 large onion, finely chopped

1 small garlic clove, crushed

1 teaspoon salt

1 teaspoon finely grated fresh ginger

1 fresh red chilli, deseeded and sliced

2 tablespoons chopped dark palm sugar (jaggery)

½ teaspoon laos (dried galangal) powder

Wash the greens very well in several changes of cold water, drain well and slice coarsely.

Put the dried shrimp in a bowl with 125 ml (4 fl oz/½ cup) hot water and leave to soak for 5 minutes. If using the brownish dried shrimp instead of the white, they will need a longer soaking time, about 25 minutes.

Put the coconut milk, onion, garlic, salt, ginger, chilli, palm sugar and laos powder into a large saucepan and bring to the boil. Add the shrimp and their soaking water, then add the kangkung. Reduce the heat to low and simmer for 20 minutes, or until tender. Serve hot with rice.

Sayur Lodeh
Vegetables in coconut sauce

Serves: 6

Any vegetables in season can be used in this dish – green beans, cabbage, cauliflower, broccoli, zucchini (courgette), pumpkin (winter squash) and bamboo shoots is an excellent combination.

500–750 g (1 lb 2 oz–1 lb 11 oz) mixed vegetables

2 tablespoons peanut oil

1 onion, finely chopped

2 garlic cloves, crushed

1 teaspoon Sambal ulek (page 104) or 1 fresh red chilli, deseeded and chopped

1 teaspoon dried shrimp paste

1 stem lemongrass or 2 strips lemon zest

1 large ripe tomato, peeled, deseeded and chopped

500 ml (17 fl oz/2 cups) vegetable stock

375 ml (12½ fl oz/1½ cups) coconut milk (pages 8–9)

3 teaspoons Peanut sauce (page 107) or peanut butter

2 teaspoons salt, or to taste

lemon juice, to taste (optional)

Slice the beans, zucchini, pumpkin and bamboo shoots into small pieces; cauliflower or broccoli should be broken or cut into florets and cabbage shredded coarsely and the shreds cut across once or twice – if they are too long it makes the dish awkward to eat.

Heat the peanut oil in a saucepan over medium heat. Add the onion and cook until it is soft and starting to colour, then add the garlic, sambal ulek and shrimp paste and cook over low heat for 2 minutes, crushing the shrimp paste with the back of a spoon and stirring well. Add the lemongrass and tomato and cook to a pulp.

Add the stock and coconut milk to the pan and bring to simmering point. Add the vegetables: simmer the beans for 4 minutes, simmer the cauliflower and broccoli for 3 minutes, then add the cabbage, zucchini, pumpkin and bamboo shoots and cook for a further 3 minutes. Stir in the peanut sauce and season with salt, to taste. A squeeze of lemon juice may be added if a sharper flavour is preferred. Serve hot.

Vegetables

Sayur Kol
Spicy cabbage in coconut milk

Serves: 6

2 onions, chopped

2 garlic cloves

2 fresh red chillies, deseeded and chopped, or 1 teaspoon chilli powder

1 teaspoon dried shrimp paste

2 teaspoons tamarind pulp

2 tablespoons peanut oil

3 daun salam leaves (glossary)

2 strips lemon zest

375 ml (12½ fl oz/1½ cups) thick coconut milk (pages 8–9)

1 teaspoon salt

500 g (1 lb 2 oz) cabbage, coarsely shredded

Put the onion, garlic and chilli into a food processor and process to a paste.

Wrap the shrimp paste in a piece of foil and roast under a preheated grill (broiler) for 5 minutes, turning halfway through the cooking time.

Soak the tamarind pulp in 60 ml (2 fl oz/¼ cup) hot water for 10 minutes. Squeeze to dissolve the pulp in the water, then strain, discarding the seeds and fibre.

Heat the peanut oil in a wok or large heavy-based saucepan over medium heat. Add the daun salam leaves and cook for 1 minute, then stir in the chilli mixture and the shrimp paste and cook, stirring regularly, until the mixture darkens. Add the lemon zest, coconut milk and salt and bring to a simmer, stirring constantly. Add the cabbage and simmer for 3–4 minutes, or until the cabbage is cooked but still crisp. Stir in the tamarind liquid and serve.

Pecal Terung
Eggplant petjal

Serves: 6

2 large firm eggplants (aubergines)

1 teaspoon tamarind pulp

1½ tablespoons peanut oil

5 candlenuts or brazil nuts

1 teaspoon dried shrimp paste

½ teaspoon laos (dried galangal) powder

½ teaspoon Sambal ulek (page 104)

1 tablespoon dark soy sauce

1 teaspoon chopped dark palm sugar (jaggery)

125 ml (4 fl oz/½ cup) thick coconut milk (pages 8–9)

Peel the eggplants and cut into cubes. Drop into lightly salted boiling water or cook over steam until tender. Drain well.

Soak the tamarind pulp in 1 tablespoon hot water for 10 minutes. Squeeze to dissolve the pulp in the water, then strain, discarding the seeds and fibre.

Heat the peanut oil in a wok or small frying pan over low heat. Add the candlenuts and shrimp paste and stir constantly, crushing the shrimp paste with the back of a spoon. Add the laos powder, sambal ulek, tamarind liquid, soy sauce, palm sugar and coconut milk and continue to simmer gently until the eggplant is tender. Serve the eggplant with the warm coconut sauce poured over the top.

Sayur Tumis
Stir-fried vegetables

Serves: 4–6

Use any kind of vegetable, or a mixture of different vegetables in this stir-fry – coarsely shredded cabbage, watercress broken into bite-sized lengths, chokos that have first been peeled and sliced, green beans, bean sprouts, sliced celery, or any of your other favourites that are in season.

300 g (10½ oz/about 3 cups) mixed sliced vegetables, washed and well drained

2 tablespoons vegetable oil

1 garlic clove, crushed

1 small onion, finely chopped

4 dried daun salam leaves

¼ teaspoon dried shrimp paste

½ teaspoon salt, or to taste

1 tablespoon light soy sauce, or to taste

Heat the vegetable oil in a wok or large heavy-based frying pan over medium heat. Add the garlic, onion, daun salam leaves and shrimp paste and stir-fry until the onion is soft; crush the shrimp paste with the back of a spoon. Add the vegetables and stir-fry until lightly cooked, but still crisp. Add the salt and soy sauce, to taste and serve immediately.

Urap

Cooked vegetables with coconut

Serves: 4–6

½ teaspoon dried shrimp paste

60 g (2 oz/1 cup) freshly grated coconut or 90 g (3 oz/1 cup) desiccated (shredded) coconut soaked in 2 tablespoons hot water

1 small onion, finely chopped

½ teaspoon Sambal ulek (page 104) or chilli powder

1 teaspoon salt

2 tablespoons lemon juice

250 g (9 oz/2 cups) sliced green beans

4 carrots, cut into thin strips

180 g (6½ oz/2 cups) fresh bean sprouts, trimmed

½ small cabbage, sliced

1 bamboo shoot, thinly sliced

Wrap the shrimp paste in foil and roast under a preheated grill (broiler) for 5 minutes, turning once. Unwrap the shrimp paste and place in a bowl along with the coconut, onion, sambal ulek, salt and lemon juice, stirring well to combine.

Put all the vegetables in a steamer basket and pour the coconut mixture over the top, reserving some to use as a garnish. Steam the vegetables for 5–8 minutes, then turn out onto a serving dish and sprinkle with the reserved coconut mixture. Use as an accompaniment or as a salad in its own right.

Sayur Buncis
Bean sayur

Serves: 6

2 teaspoons tamarind pulp

2 tablespoons peanut oil

1 onion, finely chopped

2 garlic cloves, crushed

2 fresh red chillies, deseeded and chopped

1 teaspoon dried shrimp paste

1 teaspoon finely grated lemon zest

2 teaspoons ground coriander

1 teaspoon ground cumin

½ teaspoon laos (dried galangal) powder

1 teaspoon salt

6 dried daun salam leaves (glossary)

750 ml (25½ fl oz/3 cups) vegetable or chicken stock

500 g (1 lb 2 oz) fresh green beans, sliced

1 cooked boneless skinless chicken breast, diced

375 ml (12½ fl oz/1½ cups) coconut milk (pages 8–9)

Soak the tamarind pulp in 60 ml (2 fl oz/¼ cup) hot water for 10 minutes. Squeeze to dissolve the pulp in the water, then strain, discarding the seeds and fibre. Measure 2 tablespoons of the liquid and set aside.

Heat the peanut oil in a wok or large heavy-based frying pan over medium heat. Add the onion, garlic, chilli and shrimp paste and cook for 5 minutes, stirring and crushing the shrimp paste with the back of a spoon. Add the lemon zest and ground spices and cook for 1 minute, then add the salt, tamarind liquid, daun salam leaves, stock and beans. Bring to the boil, simmer for 8 minutes, then add the chicken and coconut milk and continue simmering for 5 minutes, or until heated through.

Note

Rice vermicelli (rice-stick) noodles can be added to this sayur when it is the main dish. Soak 125 g (4½ oz) rice vermicelli noodles in very hot water for 10 minutes, and drain well. Add to sayur and cook for a further 2 minutes.

Tahu Goreng Kecap
Fried tofu with soy sauce

Serves: 6

60 ml (2 fl oz/¼ cup) dark soy sauce

1 tablespoon chopped dark palm sugar (jaggery)

1 onion, roughly chopped

1 teaspoon Sambal ulek (page 104) or 1 fresh red chilli, deseeded and chopped

1 garlic clove

oil for deep-frying

380 g (13½ oz) pressed firm tofu, cut into cubes

90 g (3 oz/1 cup) fresh bean sprouts, trimmed

4 spring onions (scallions), thinly sliced, to garnish

To make the sauce, put the soy sauce, palm sugar, onion, sambal ulek and garlic in a food processor and process until smooth. If a less pungent sauce is preferred, make one as in the recipe for Tofu omelettes (page 64).

Heat the oil in a wok or large heavy-based saucepan over medium heat. When the oil is hot, deep-fry the tofu, in batches, taking care not to break it, until browned on all sides. Drain on paper towel, then arrange on a serving plate. Top with the bean sprouts and garnish with the spring onion. Spoon over the sauce and serve.

Gado-Gado
Vegetables with peanut sauce

Serves: 6–8

1 telegraph (long) cucumber

1 small bunch watercress

500 g (1 lb 2 oz/4 cups) sliced green beans

3 carrots, cut into thin strips

½ small cabbage, sliced

3 large potatoes, boiled, peeled and thinly sliced

205 g (7 oz/2¼ cups) fresh bean sprouts, trimmed

3 hard-boiled eggs, peeled and quartered

Peanut sauce (page 107)

Score the skin of the cucumber with a fork and cut into very thin slices. Wash the watercress and break into sprigs, discarding the tough stalks. Refrigerate until needed.

Cook the beans and carrot in lightly salted boiling water until just tender – the beans should still be crisp to bite and the carrot should be tender.

Blanch the cabbage in salted boiling water for 1–2 minutes, or until tender but not limp. Drain and refresh under cold water.

Put the watercress on a large platter and arrange the various vegetables and the bean sprouts in separate sections on top. Surround with slices of cucumber, with the egg quarters in the centre. Serve cold, accompanied by the peanut sauce, which is spooned over individual servings.

Sayur Kari
Vegetables cooked in coconut milk with curry spices

Serves: 6

2 tablespoons peanut oil

2 onions, finely chopped

2 fresh red chillies, deseeded and sliced

4 garlic cloves, finely chopped

2 teaspoons finely grated fresh ginger

2 teaspoons ground coriander

1 teaspoon ground cumin

1 teaspoon ground turmeric

1 teaspoon freshly ground black pepper

½ teaspoon laos (dried galangal) powder

2 stems lemongrass or 1 teaspoon finely
   grated lemon zest

½ teaspoon dried shrimp paste

125 g (4½ oz) rump steak, finely diced

1 litre (34 fl oz/4 cups) beef stock

500 ml (17 fl oz/2 cups) thick coconut milk
   (pages 8–9)

2½ teaspoons salt

6 dried daun salam leaves (glossary)

2 large potatoes, peeled and diced

250 g (9 oz) green beans, finely sliced

500 g (1 lb 2 oz) cabbage, coarsely shredded

125 g (4½ oz) rice vermicelli (rice-stick)
   noodles, soaked in hot water for
   10 minutes and drained

lemon juice, to taste

Heat the peanut oil in a wok or large heavy-based saucepan over medium heat. Add the onion and chilli and cook until the onion is soft and starting to colour. Add the garlic and ginger and cook for 1 minute, then add the ground spices, lemongrass and shrimp paste and stir-fry for a further 1 minute. Add the beef and stir-fry for 3–4 minutes, or until the beef changes colour. Add the stock, coconut milk, salt and daun salam leaves and bring slowly to the boil, stirring occasionally. Add the potato and simmer for 10 minutes, then add the beans and simmer for 5 minutes. Add the cabbage, return to the boil, then add the vermicelli and simmer 2–3 minutes. Remove from the heat and add the lemon juice to taste. Serve immediately.

Pacari
Pineapple coconut curry

Serves: 6

- 1 small pineapple, not too ripe
- 1 tablespoon oil
- 1 small onion, finely chopped
- 1 garlic clove, finely chopped
- 1 small cinnamon stick
- 3 whole cloves
- 3 cardamom pods, bruised
- 1 teaspoon ground coriander
- 1½ teaspoons ground cumin
- ½ teaspoon chilli powder or 1 fresh red chilli, deseeded and sliced
- 1 teaspoon salt
- 250 ml (8½ fl oz/1 cup) thick coconut milk (pages 8–9)
- 1 teaspoon chopped dark palm sugar (jaggery)

Peel the pineapple with a sharp knife, remove the eyes and cut into quarters lengthways, removing the hard core. Cut each quarter in half lengthways, then into thick slices crossways.

Heat the oil in a wok or large heavy-based frying pan over medium heat. Add the onion, garlic and whole spices and cook until the onion is soft. Add the coriander, cumin, chilli powder and salt and stir for a few minutes, or until the spices have browned. Add the pineapple and stir well to coat. Add the coconut milk and palm sugar and bring to simmering point, stirring constantly. Simmer for 3–4 minutes, or until the pineapple is just tender, but not too soft. Serve hot.

Tahu Goreng Kacang
Fried tofu with peanuts

Serves: 4

1 teaspoon tamarind pulp

peanut oil for frying

380 g (13½ oz) pressed firm tofu, cut into cubes

peanut oil for frying

80 g (2¾ oz/½ cup) raw peanuts

1 large garlic clove, crushed

½ teaspoon dried shrimp paste

140 g (5 oz/½ cup) crushed roasted peanuts or crunchy peanut butter

2 tablespoons dark soy sauce

½ teaspoon Sambal ulek (page 104)

1 teaspoon chopped dark palm sugar (jaggery)

125 ml (4 fl oz/½ cup) coconut milk (pages 8–9)

75 g (2¾ oz/1 cup) shredded cabbage

90 g (3 oz/1 cup) fresh bean sprouts, trimmed

4 spring onions (scallions), thinly sliced, to garnish

Soak the tamarind pulp in 1 tablespoon hot water for 10 minutes. Squeeze to dissolve the pulp in the water, then strain, discarding the seeds and fibre. Set aside.

Heat the peanut oil in a wok or large heavy-based frying pan over medium heat. Add the tofu, taking care not to break it up, and cook until golden brown on all sides. Drain on paper towel.

In the same wok, cook the raw peanuts for 3–4 minutes, then drain well and rub off the skins. Set aside.

Make the sauce by pouring off all but 1 tablespoon of oil from the wok. Add the garlic and shrimp paste and cook over low heat, stirring constantly, and crushing the shrimp paste with the back of a spoon. Add the crushed peanuts, soy sauce, tamarind liquid, sambal ulek and palm sugar and stir until well combined. Remove from the heat and gradually add the coconut milk, stirring until the sauce is a thick pouring consistency.

To serve, put the tofu on a serving plate, cover with the shredded cabbage and bean sprouts. Spoon the sauce over the top and garnish with the spring onion and fried peanuts.

Accompaniments

❀

Sambalan
Basic sambal seasoning

Makes: 2 cups

If you like hot food you will find it useful to make up a quantity of this base, which you can cook and keep bottled in the refrigerator ready to add to boiled or fried potatoes, breadfruit, yams or other starchy vegetables; hard-boiled eggs; stir-fried tofu, fish, prawns (shrimp) or other shellfish; and crisp-fried strips of meat or liver. There is no end to the variations on this theme.

2 tablespoons tamarind pulp

15–20 large dried red chillies

3 large onions, roughly chopped

8 garlic cloves

2 teaspoons dried shrimp paste

125 ml (4 fl oz/½ cup) peanut oil

3 teaspoons salt

2 tablespoons chopped dark palm sugar
  (jaggery)

Soak the tamarind pulp in 250 ml (8½ fl oz/1 cup) hot water for 10 minutes. Squeeze to dissolve the pulp in the water, then strain, discarding the seeds and fibre. Set aside.

Soak the chillies in hot water for 20 minutes.

Put the chillies and their soaking liquid into a food processor with the onion, garlic, shrimp paste and just enough of the peanut oil to combine to a smooth paste – you may need to use more than half the oil, depending on the size and shape of the blender.

Heat the remaining oil in a wok or large heavy-based frying pan over medium heat. Add the chilli paste and cook, stirring constantly, until the mixture darkens in colour and the oil separates. Wash out the blender container with the tamarind liquid and add to the wok with the salt and palm sugar, and simmer for a few minutes longer, stirring. Remove from the heat and cool, then pour into a sterilised airtight jar and refrigerate for up to 1 month.

Heat the required amount (approximately 1 tablespoon to 250 g/9 oz of the main ingredient) and stir-fry the already cooked main ingredient in it briefly. If a sauce is required, add 125–250 ml (4–8½ fl oz/½–1 cup) thick coconut milk (pages 8–9) and heat to simmering point, stirring constantly.

Accompaniments

Sambal Kepala Udang
Hot–sour prawn head sambal

Serves: 4

....

This is one of the by-products using the tastiest part of the prawn (shrimp) – the head. It contains most of the fat and therefore most of the flavour. While it may not be the easiest thing to swallow, it is worth chewing on (and politely discarding) just to savour the combination of flavours.

....

heads from 500 g (1 lb 2 oz) raw prawns (shrimp)

2 teaspoons tamarind pulp

2 tablespoons peanut oil

5–6 curry leaves

1 onion, finely chopped

1 large garlic clove, crushed

½ teaspoon finely grated fresh ginger

1 teaspoon Sambal ulek (page 104) or 2 fresh red chillies, deseeded and chopped

1 teaspoon dried shrimp paste

1 teaspoon ground coriander

½ teaspoon ground cumin

½ teaspoon salt

Wash the prawn heads well and remove the hard, armour-like shell, the long thin feelers and the eyes. Drain well in a colander and then pat dry on paper towel.

Soak the tamarind pulp in 60 ml (2 fl oz/¼ cup) hot water for 10 minutes. Squeeze to dissolve the pulp in the water, then strain, discarding the seeds and fibre. Set aside.

Heat the peanut oil in a wok or small heavy-based frying pan over medium heat. Add the curry leaves and cook for a few seconds, then add the onion, garlic and ginger and cook until the onion is soft and starts to brown. Add the sambal ulek and the shrimp paste, crushing it with the back of a spoon. Continue cooking for 3 minutes, stirring regularly, then add the coriander and cumin and cook for 1 minute longer. Add the prawn heads and stir-fry for 2–3 minutes, then add the tamarind liquid and salt. Reduce the heat to low and simmer until the liquid evaporates completely and the prawn heads start to sizzle in the oil, about 10–15 minutes. Serve as a tasty side dish with rice and curries.

Sambal Goreng Udang Asam
Piquant fried prawn sambal

Serves: 6

1½ tablespoons tamarind pulp

2 tablespoons peanut oil

1 onion, finely chopped

3 garlic cloves, finely chopped

½ teaspoon finely grated fresh ginger

2 teaspoons Sambal ulek (page 104) or
    4 fresh red chillies

½ teaspoon laos (dried galangal) powder

1 stem lemongrass or 2 strips thinly peeled
    lemon zest

500 g (1 lb 2 oz) raw small prawns (shrimp),
    peeled, deveined and chopped

1 teaspoon salt

1 teaspoon chopped dark palm sugar
    (jaggery), or to taste

Soak the tamarind pulp in 80 ml (2½ fl oz/⅓ cup) hot water for 10 minutes. Squeeze to dissolve the pulp in the water, then strain, discarding the seeds and fibre. Set aside.

Heat the peanut oil in a frying pan over medium heat. Add the onion, garlic and ginger and cook until the onion is soft and starts to turn golden. Add the sambal ulek, laos powder and lemongrass, then add the prawns and cook, stirring constantly, until the prawns change colour. Add the tamarind liquid and simmer over low heat until the sauce has thickened and the oil starts to separate. Discard the lemongrass and stir in the salt and palm sugar, to taste. Serve as a side dish to rice and curries.

Sambal Buncis
Green bean sambal

Serves: 6

1 tablespoon peanut oil

250 g (9 oz/2 cups) sliced green beans

1 tablespoon crushed garlic

½ teaspoon Sambal ulek (page 104)

½ teaspoon salt, or to taste

1 small onion, finely sliced

Heat the peanut oil in a wok or large heavy-based frying pan over high heat. Add the beans and toss in the oil for 2 minutes, then add the garlic and stir-fry for 1 minute. Add the sambal ulek and salt and stir-fry for 1 minute further – the beans should be tender but still crisp. Remove from the heat, mix in the onion and serve as an accompaniment to a rice and curry meal.

Sambal Ulek
Hot chilli paste

Makes: 1 cup

Sambal ulek and Sambal bajak (page 112) may be purchased in jars from Asian grocery stores, but they are simple enough to make at home and can be stored for weeks in the refrigerator.

25 fresh red chillies

vinegar or tamarind liquid

2 teaspoons salt

Put the chillies, seeds and all, into a food processor with just enough vinegar or tamarind liquid to keep the mass moving and blend to a paste. Add the salt, to taste. Pour into a sterilised airtight jar and store in the refrigerator for up to 1 month.

Telur Berwarna
Marbled eggs

Makes: 6

The Southeast Asian love of bright colours is reflected in this favourite garnish for a festive meal. Employing the method used by the Chinese in their marbled tea eggs, Indonesians give hard-boiled eggs a marbling of bright red, green or yellow.

6 eggs

salt

red, green and yellow food colouring

If the eggs have been refrigerated, allow them to come to room temperature. Put them gently in a saucepan with enough cold, salted water to cover, and bring to simmering point, stirring gently during the first 5 minutes to centre the yolks. When the water starts to bubble, gently cook the eggs for about 7 minutes, then cool them under cold running water. Meanwhile, put water in 3 small saucepans and use the food colouring to colour each either a deep red, green or yellow. Bring to the boil.

On a hard surface gently tap the eggs to crack the shells all over, but do not remove any part of the shell. Put 2 eggs into each pan and simmer for a further 5 minutes, then turn off the heat and allow the eggs to stand in the coloured water for at least 2 hours. When the shell is removed, there will be a bright marbling of colour on the whites of the eggs. Halve lengthways, and use as a garnish for Festive yellow rice (page 23) or other festive dishes.

Bawang Goreng
Fried onion flakes

Makes: 2 cups

Fried onion flakes are an important garnish as well as a flavouring for many Indonesian dishes. You can make these from scratch, using raw onions, or simply deep-fry pre-bought onion flakes, which are available from most large supermarkets and Asian grocery stores. If using raw onions, slice them consistently paper-thin, otherwise some will burn while others will be uncooked.

500 g (1 lb 2 oz) shallots or onions, very
  thinly sliced, or dried onion flakes

500 ml (17 fl oz/2 cups) peanut or
  vegetable oil for deep-frying

If using raw onions, place them in a wok with enough cold oil to cover and heat slowly over medium heat. Let the onion cook until deep brown, but not black. Lift out, drain on paper towel and cool. Keep the strained oil for cooking stir-fries or fried rice, as it is deliciously flavoursome.

If using pre-bought onion flakes, heat the oil in a wok or large heavy-based saucepan over medium heat. When the oil is hot, lower the dried onion flakes on a wire strainer into the hot oil and deep-fry for a few seconds until they turn golden brown. Lift them out immediately and drain on paper towel to cool. Store the fried onion flakes in an airtight container for up to 2 weeks.

Accompaniments

Pisang Goreng
Fried bananas

Serves: 6

These fried bananas are served as an accompaniment to rice and curries.

6 medium or 3 large bananas, ripe but quite firm

oil for frying

salt for sprinkling

Peel the bananas, and if they are large, cut in half crossways. Smaller bananas can be cut down the centre lengthways.

Heat a little oil in a frying pan over medium–high heat. Add the bananas and cook until brown all over – turn the bananas carefully, as they will break easily when hot. Lift out onto a small plate to serve, and sprinkle lightly with salt.

Krupuk Emping
Fried melinjo nut wafers

These flattened-out kernels of the melinjo nut are sold in packets in Asian grocery stores and only require a few seconds frying in hot oil.

oil for deep-frying

melinjo nuts

Heat the oil in a wok or large heavy-based saucepan over medium heat. When the oil is hot, deep-fry the melinjo nuts, in batches, spooning the oil over them as they cook, which should take less than 1 minute – do not let them get more than light brown or they will be bitter. Lift them out quickly using a slotted spoon and drain on paper towel. Sprinkle lightly with salt before serving as an accompaniment to a meal or as a nibble with drinks.

Saus Kacang (1)
Crunchy peanut sauce

Makes: 3 cups

There are many recipes for peanut sauce, but this is my favourite. Without the addition of liquid, it keeps for weeks. When required, add three parts coconut milk (pages 8–9) or water to one part sauce and re-heat.

140 ml (4½ fl oz) peanut oil

1 teaspoon dried garlic flakes

2 tablespoons dried onion flakes

2 large dried red chillies

1 teaspoon dried shrimp paste

1 tablespoon lemon juice

1 tablespoon dark soy sauce or kecap manis

375 g (13 oz/1½ cups) crunchy peanut butter

1½ tablespoons chopped dark palm sugar (jaggery)

Heat the peanut oil in a wok or heavy-based saucepan over medium heat. Put the garlic flakes into a wire strainer, lower into the hot oil and deep-fry for a few seconds until golden. Lift out and drain on paper towel. Deep-fry the onion flakes in the same way. Drain on paper towel and set aside to cool.

Deep-fry the whole chillies until they are puffed and crisp, which should take less than 1 minute. Remove from the wok, drain on paper towel and cool. Discard the stalks and seeds and crumble or chop the chillies into small pieces. Set aside.

Add the shrimp paste to the remaining oil in the wok, crushing it with the back of a spoon. Add the lemon juice and kecap manis, then remove from the heat and stir in the peanut butter until well combined. Allow to cool.

Stir the fried garlic and onion flakes, crumbled chilli and palm sugar into the peanut mixture. Store in a sterilised airtight jar for up to 1 month. Use as is, or mix in enough coconut milk or water to make a more liquid sauce, adding salt to taste.

Note

Fresh garlic and onion can be used instead of dried garlic and onion flakes. Peel 6 garlic cloves and cut into thin slices. Peel and finely slice 1 onion. Fry separately over low heat, removing from the heat as soon as they turn golden brown. Drain on paper towel and cool. Crumble the crisp garlic slices before adding to the sauce.

Accompaniments

Rujak Buah-Buah Pedis
Spicy fruit salad

Serves: 6–8

1 grapefruit or pomelo fruit, peeled

1 orange or mandarin, peeled

2 tart green apples, peeled and thinly sliced

1 cucumber, peeled and diced

1 small pineapple, peeled and diced

½ teaspoon dried shrimp paste

½ teaspoon Sambal ulek (page 104)

1 tablespoon chopped dark palm sugar (jaggery)

1 tablespoon kecap manis

2 tablespoons lemon juice

Break up the grapefruit and orange, cutting between the membranes to release the segments and remove the seeds – do this over a bowl, saving any juices. Place in a serving bowl with the apple, cucumber and pineapple.

Wrap the shrimp paste in foil and roast under a preheated grill (broiler) for 5 minutes, turning once. Unwrap the shrimp paste and put in a bowl along with the sambal ulek, palm sugar, kecap manis and lemon juice, stirring well to combine. Pour over the fruit and toss well to coat. Allow to stand for a few minutes before serving.

Saus Kacang Pedis
Hot peanut sauce

Makes: 2 cups

60 ml (2 fl oz/¼ cup) peanut oil

1 tablespoon dried onion flakes

1 garlic clove, crushed

¼ teaspoon dried shrimp paste

4 fresh red chillies, deseeded and chopped or 2 teaspoons Sambal ulek (page 104)

80 g (2¾ oz) smooth or crunchy peanut butter

½ teaspoon salt

1 tablespoon kecap manis

2 teaspoons grated dark palm sugar (jaggery)

1 tablespoon lemon juice

Heat the peanut oil in a wok or small heavy-based frying pan over medium heat. Add the onion flakes and cook briefly until they turn golden. Drain on paper towel and set aside.

Leave about 2 tablespoons of the oil in the wok and cook the garlic, shrimp paste and chilli for 1 minute over low heat, crushing the shrimp paste with the back of a spoon. Add the peanut butter and 190 ml (6½ fl oz/¾ cup) water and stir until well combined. Remove from the heat and add the salt, kecap manis, palm sugar and lemon juice. If necessary, add more water to make it a thick pouring consistency. Remove from the heat and allow to cool, then crumble the onion flakes into the sauce and stir well. Serve at room temperature.

Saus Kacang (2)
Mild peanut sauce

Makes: 2 cups

125 g (4½ oz/½ cup) smooth or crunchy peanut butter

¾ teaspoon garlic salt

2 teaspoons chopped dark palm sugar (jaggery)

2 tablespoons dark soy sauce

lemon juice, to taste

½ teaspoon dried shrimp paste (optional)

coconut milk (pages 8–9), or extra water, for thinning

Put the peanut butter and 250 ml (8½ fl oz/1 cup) water in a saucepan and stir over low heat until well combined. Remove from the heat and add the remaining ingredients, stirring well. Add just enough coconut milk or water to make the paste a thick pouring consistency. Season with salt and more lemon juice, if needed.

Serundeng (1)

Crisp spiced coconut with peanuts (quick method)

Makes: 2 cups

....

45 g (1½ oz/½ cup) desiccated (shredded) coconut

½ teaspoon dried garlic flakes

2 tablespoons dried onion flakes

½ teaspoon ground coriander

½ teaspoon ground cumin

½ teaspoon salt

80 g (2¾ oz/½ cup) roasted unsalted peanuts

In a dry frying pan stir the coconut over medium–low heat until golden. Add the garlic and onion flakes, crushing the onion flakes into small pieces first. Stir and cook until the coconut is deep golden and the garlic and onion flakes are toasted. Add the coriander, cumin and salt, stir well, then remove from the heat and allow to cool before stirring in the peanuts. This can be stored in an airtight container for up to 3 weeks.

Serundeng (2)

Crisp spiced coconut with peanuts

Makes: 2 cups

....

1 teaspoon tamarind pulp

90 g (3 oz/1 cup) desiccated (shredded) coconut

1 small onion, very finely chopped

1 garlic clove, crushed

1 teaspoon finely grated fresh ginger

2 tablespoons peanut oil

½ teaspoon dried shrimp paste

1 teaspoon ground coriander

1 teaspoon ground cumin

1 teaspoon salt

160 g (5½ oz/1 cup) roasted unsalted peanuts

Soak the tamarind pulp in 1 tablespoon hot water for 10 minutes. Squeeze to dissolve the pulp in the water, then strain, discarding the seeds and fibre. Set aside.

In a bowl, combine the coconut, onion, garlic and ginger.

Heat the peanut oil in a wok or large heavy-based frying pan over low heat. Add the shrimp paste, crushing it with the back of a spoon, and cook for 1–2 minutes. Add the coconut mixture and stir constantly until the coconut is golden brown. Add the coriander, cumin, salt and tamarind liquid and cook until the coconut is dry and crisp, stirring often. This takes quite a while and cannot be hurried by raising the heat. Allow to cool, then mix in the peanuts. Serve with a rice meal, or use as a garnish.

Sambal Bajak

Fried chilli sambal

Makes: 1 cup

Cooled, then stored in an airtight jar, this sambal will keep for weeks in the refrigerator. When serving, use a teaspoon for portions and warn guests it should be eaten in tiny quantities with rice, not by itself. As a taste for sambal is acquired, it is enjoyed on crisp crackers, in sandwiches, on steaks; in fact there is no limit to the ways a sambal addict will use it.

6 large fresh red chillies, roughly chopped

1 large onion, roughly chopped

6 garlic cloves

1 tablespoon tamarind pulp

60 ml (2 fl oz/¼ cup) peanut oil

8 candlenuts or brazil nuts, finely grated

½ teaspoon laos (dried galangal) powder

1 tablespoon dried shrimp paste

1 teaspoon salt

2 tablespoons chopped dark palm sugar (jaggery)

Put the chilli, onion and garlic in a food processor and process to a pulp – it might be necessary to stop and start the motor several times to draw the onion and chilli down on to the blades.

Soak the tamarind pulp in 125 ml (4 fl oz/½ cup) hot water for 10 minutes. Squeeze to dissolve the pulp in the water, then strain, discarding the seeds and fibre. Measure out 100 ml (3½ fl oz) of the tamarind liquid and set aside.

Heat the peanut oil in a small frying pan over low heat. Add the chilli mixture and cook for 5 minutes, stirring constantly, until well cooked but not brown. Add the candlenuts, laos powder, shrimp paste and salt, crushing the shrimp paste with the back of a spoon and stirring until the mixture is well blended. Add the tamarind liquid and palm sugar, stir well, and simmer until reddish-brown in colour and the oil starts to separate. Remove from the heat, allow to cool, then pour into a sterilised airtight jar and refrigerate for up to 2 weeks.

Note

If a food processor is not available, seed the chillies and chop very finely. Peel and finely chop the onion and crush the garlic with salt, before cooking.

Sweets
and
Desserts

❁

Spekkoek Kueh Lapis
Many-layered spice cake

Makes: one 20 cm (8 in) round or square cake

This fascinating cake is not difficult to make, but you do need patience for the special cooking method. The layers, each hardly thicker than a wafer, are baked and then grilled (broiled) one at a time. Be prepared to hover over the oven for a couple of hours – preferably when the weather is cold enough to make this a comfortable occupation! Some people prefer a light-textured cake, while others prefer a pudding-like texture which is richer and sweeter. If the former is to your taste use the recipe as printed. But if you prefer a sweeter, moist cake that most Indonesians consider the acme of their sweetmeats, then use only 75 g (2¾ oz/½ cup) plain (all-purpose) flour and four egg whites instead of eight. The cake is served in very small, thin slices as it is so rich.

10 egg yolks

345 g (12 oz/1½ cups) caster (superfine) sugar

250 g (9 oz) butter, plus extra, melted (optional)

2 teaspoons natural vanilla extract

8 egg whites

225 g (8 oz/1½ cups) plain (all-purpose) flour, sifted

1 teaspoon ground cinnamon

1 teaspoon freshly grated nutmeg

1 teaspoon ground cardamom

½ teaspoon ground cloves

Whisk the egg yolks with 115 g (4 oz/½ cup) of the sugar in the bowl of an electric mixer, until thick and light.

Cream the butter with 170 g (6 oz/¾ cup) of the sugar and the vanilla extract until light and smooth.

In a clean, dry bowl, whisk the egg whites until stiff peaks form, then add the remaining sugar and whisk again until glossy.

Mix the egg yolk and butter mixtures together well. Fold in the flour, then the egg whites. Divide the mixture into 2 almost equal portions and mix the ground spices into the larger portion.

Preheat the oven to 160°C (320°F). Lightly grease a 20 cm (8 in) spring-form cake tin with softened butter and line the base with buttered baking paper. Dust with flour, shaking out any excess.

Put ⅓ cup of the spiced cake batter into the tin and spread with a spatula – tap the tin firmly on the work surface to help the batter spread thinly and evenly. Bake in the centre of the oven until firm, about 10 minutes.

Meanwhile, preheat the grill (broiler) and place the tin under it for 30–40 seconds, about 15 cm (6 in) away from the heat, until the top is evenly browned. Watch carefully so it does not burn – a dark coffee colour is what you should aim for.

Spread the same amount of plain (unspiced) batter over the first baked layer, return to the oven and cook for 10 minutes, then place under the grill as before. Continue with this layering until all the batter has been used, alternating the spice and plain layers and spreading the batter as thin as possible.

The extra melted butter is for those who like a really buttery cake, and is used to brush lightly over each layer after it has been grilled and before the next layer of batter is spread over.

When the last layer has been baked, insert a skewer in the centre. It should emerge slightly buttery, but not with uncooked batter clinging to it; bake for a few minutes longer if necessary. Remove from the oven and cool on a wire rack, then remove the side of the tin and cut into thin slices to serve.

Malaysia

Malaysia is a lush, green country, typical of the monsoon lands of Southeast Asia. Because of its local produce and various cooking styles it has much to offer in adventurous eating. The cooking styles include Malay, Indonesian, Indian, Chinese and Sri Lankan, for people from all these countries have settled in Malaysia. Malaysian food is very similar to some Indonesian dishes, and in both countries the languages are almost identical.

In predominantly Muslim Malaysia the food is rich and spicy. Many kinds of meat and fish are used, but never pork – it is considered unclean, and it would be a serious faux pas to offer it to anyone of the Muslim faith. Among the Chinese it is used, and is one of their favourite meats. The Hindus do not eat beef, for cattle are sacred to them.

One of the most fascinating meals I had in Malaysia was in Kuala Lumpur, at a *makan malam* or night food stall. These indoor/outdoor eating places come to life when the sun goes down. Perambulating food shops are set up, each one specialising in a particular dish. I sampled chicken satay skewers that tasted of spices and fresh lemongrass, and were served with a peanut sauce, and *ketupat*, pressed rice cakes cooked in small woven baskets of coconut palm fronds. The sauce was surprisingly mild, being quite heavily sweetened to balance the spices. I then ordered a spicy noodle soup with cockles; *sotong kangkong*, a rich, red sauce with squid and fresh greens. Next on the menu was *poh pia*, a sort of unfried spring roll (page 174 in the Singapore chapter). All this was followed by a couple of unusual sweets. *Ice kacang* came in a tall glass packed half full with shaved ice doused in a sweet red syrup with cooked and sweetened corn kernels and red beans added. Evaporated milk was poured over, turning pink as it mixed with the coloured syrup and making a drink rather than a sweet.

Just as intriguing as the food we ate was the method of ordering. As soon as we sat at the table we were surrounded by half a dozen young boys who acted as waiters for the numerous stalls surrounding the dining area. Each represented a different chef. There was no printed menu; instead they chanted the names of the dishes available from the chef they worked for. It is decidedly different from anything a Western city has to offer, but adds greatly to the charm of this friendly land.

Another experience I will not forget was an early-morning visit to an open-air market where the baskets were piled high with fresh, shiny chillies of all shapes and sizes and ranging from bright green through yellow and orange to vivid scarlet; bundles of green and white lemongrass and other herbs; eggplants (aubergines) in amazing variety – green, purple, white, large, small, round or long, and one variety only as large as a pea. Everything looked so tempting that I had to restrain myself from a mad buying spree. I did succumb, however, to large bunches of fresh rambutan – those bright red, oval fruit the size of a pullet's egg and covered with fleshy hairs which give them a bizarre appearance. When the skin is removed (it is thin and soft enough to be peeled by a thumb nail) there is a translucent white-fleshed fruit inside looking very much like a lychee. The flavour is refreshingly sweet-sour. It was in Malaysia too that I ate the best star fruit I have ever tasted. After tasting the fruit – so deeply golden and full of flavour – it quite changed my opinion of star fruit as being only a thirst quencher or table decoration.

Serving and eating a Malaysian meal

To save space, I would like to refer you to the Indonesian chapter, for what has been written about Indonesian food applies to true Malay food. In addition, Malaysian cooks take pride in their rich korma and biriani, which the Indian settlers brought with them and which have become part of the local culinary scene. Food is traditionally eaten with the fingers, but nowadays a spoon and fork is considered more refined. However, on family and ceremonial occasions people revert to the old ways.

Unlike many Asian countries where desserts are not often served, Malays love rich, sweet desserts and these are based on sago, mung beans, bean flour or glutinous rice. Palm sugar (jaggery) is added for sweetness, coconut milk for richness and pandanus leaf, the Asian equivalent of the vanilla bean, for flavour. In some recipes the sweet spices such as cardamom, cinnamon and cloves are used.

Utensils

The Malaysian version of the wok is the *kuali* – shaped the same, but generally thicker and heavier. In the absence of the clay pots (*blangah*) which are favoured for cooking curries, stainless-steel or heavy-based saucepans are recommended, especially for dishes using a large proportion of coconut milk, which discolours in an iron *kuali*. A deep frying pan is useful, and while the grinding stone (*batu giling*) features largely in preparing Malaysian spices, an electric spice grinder or food processor will do this job in a Western kitchen.

Your Malaysian shelf

This is a list of spices, sauces, sambals and other flavourings which are often used in Malaysian cooking and good to have on hand to make the recipes in this chapter.

candlenuts or brazil nuts

coconut, desiccated (shredded) or freshly grated

coconut cream and milk (pages 8–9)

coriander, ground

cumin, ground

curry leaves

daun salam leaves

dried prawn (shrimp) powder

dried shrimp

dried shrimp paste

galangal, fresh or brined

glutinous rice (pulot)

kecap manis (sweet dark soy sauce) or use dark soy sauce

kencur (aromatic ginger) powder

laos (dried galangal) powder

palm sugar (jaggery), or use soft or dark brown sugar

pandanus leaves

peanut oil

salted soy beans (taucheo)

sambal bajak (page 112)

sambal ulek (page 104)

sereh powder (dried ground lemongrass)

sesame oil

shrimp sauce

soy sauce

tamarind pulp

turmeric, ground

Note

Though fresh galangal may look similar to ginger, this rhizome is infinitely harder to cut. Sliced, it adds flavour simply by simmering in soups and sauces, but for a curry paste, the rhizome will need to be peeled and finely chopped before grinding with a mortar and pestle with other ingredients. If you do not have access to the fresh root, sliced galangal in brine is the next best option. Otherwise, use the dry ground spice, known as laos powder. It will imbue the food with the correct flavour note, though perhaps with a little less of the lively zing delivered by the fresh rhizome.

Rice,
Noodles
and Soups

❖

Nasi Kunyit
Glutinous yellow rice

Serves: 6

450 g (1 lb/2¼ cups) glutinous rice (pulot)

2 teaspoons salt

1 garlic clove, crushed

1 teaspoon ground turmeric

½ teaspoon freshly ground black pepper

1 pandanus leaf

500 ml (17 fl oz/2 cups) hot coconut milk (pages 8–9)

Fried onion flakes (page 105), to serve

Wash the rice well and drain in a colander for 30 minutes.

Put the rice into a saucepan with 500 ml (17 fl oz/2 cups) water. Add the salt, garlic, turmeric, pepper and pandanus leaf for flavouring. Bring to the boil, then reduce the heat to low, cover, and steam for 10 minutes. Uncover, add the coconut milk (which should be very hot) and stir gently with a fork. Re-cover and cook for a further 10 minutes or until the rice is tender. Serve the rice garnished with the onion flakes.

Sothi
Coconut milk soup

Serves: 6

This soup is spooned over boiled rice, not served as a first course by itself.

500 ml (17 fl oz/2 cups) thin coconut milk (pages 8–9)

2 onions, thinly sliced

6 curry leaves

2 fresh red or green chillies, deseeded

½ teaspoon ground turmeric

1½ teaspoons salt

2 tablespoons dried prawn (shrimp) powder

375 ml (12½ fl oz/1½ cups) thick coconut milk (pages 8–9)

2 tablespoons lemon juice

Put all the ingredients, except the thick coconut milk and lemon juice, into a saucepan and bring to the boil. Reduce the heat to low and simmer for 15 minutes. Add the thick coconut milk and continue to stir as the soup re-heats to prevent it from curdling. Remove from the heat, stir in the lemon juice and serve as an accompaniment to rice and a dry curry.

Ketupat
Compressed rice cakes

Serves: 6

These firm rice cakes are usually cooked in individual baskets of woven coconut leaves so that the rice swells until it fills the basket and becomes firmly compressed. This is a way of producing similar results in Western kitchens.

415 g (14½ oz/2¼ cups) short- or medium-grain rice

banana leaf or aluminium foil

Wash the rice well and drain in a colander for 30 minutes.

Put the rice into a saucepan with 1 litre (34 fl oz/4 cups) water and bring to the boil. Reduce the heat to low, cover, and cook for 30–40 minutes, or until all the water is absorbed. Stir vigorously with a wooden spoon, then press the rice into a cake tin or baking dish to a depth of about 2.5 cm (1 in). Use a piece of washed and oiled banana leaf or oiled foil to cover the surface of the rice and then place a plate on top and press down firmly. Put a weight on top and leave at room temperature for at least 2 hours, or until very firm.

Remove the weight, plate and banana leaf, and use a wet knife to cut the rice into 5 cm (2 in) squares.

Rice, Noodles and Soups

Char Kway Teow
Fried rice noodles

Serves: 6–8

80 ml (2½ fl oz/⅓ cup) oil or lard

2 garlic cloves, finely chopped

4 small onions, sliced

4 fresh red chillies, deseeded and chopped

125 g (4½ oz) barbecued pork, thinly sliced

250 g (9 oz) raw small prawns (shrimp),
    peeled and deveined

250 g (9 oz) small squid tubes (optional),
    cleaned and thinly sliced

2 Chinese sausages (lap cheong), steamed
    and thinly sliced

90 g (3 oz/1 cup) fresh bean sprouts,
    trimmed

1 kg (2 lb 3 oz) fresh rice noodles, sliced
    into 5 mm (¼ in) strips

2 tablespoons dark soy sauce

2 tablespoons light soy sauce

1 tablespoon oyster sauce

3 eggs, lightly beaten

salt and freshly ground black pepper,
    to taste

4 spring onions (scallions), chopped

Heat 2 tablespoons of the oil in a wok or large heavy-based frying pan and cook the garlic, onion and chilli over medium heat, stirring, until the onion is soft. Add the pork, prawns, squid, if using, and Chinese sausage and stir-fry for 2–3 minutes, or until all the seafood is cooked through. Add the bean sprouts and toss once or twice, then remove to a plate.

Heat the remaining oil in the wok and add the rice noodles, stirring constantly until heated through. Add the soy sauce and oyster sauce and toss well to combine. Add the egg and stir constantly until it is set. Return the seafood and pork to the wok and toss to combine and heat through. Season with salt and freshly ground black pepper, to taste, and serve hot, garnished with the spring onion.

Note

Fresh rice noodles are sold at Asian grocery stores, and are known as sa hor fun.

Sayur Udang Bayam

Prawn and spinach soup

Serves: 6

250 g (9 oz) raw prawns (shrimp), peeled, deveined and finely chopped (heads and shells reserved for stock)

60 ml (2 fl oz/¼ cup) peanut oil

1 onion, thinly sliced

1–2 fresh red chillies, deseeded and sliced

1 garlic clove, crushed

½ teaspoon ground turmeric

1 small bunch English spinach or silverbeet (Swiss chard), leaves and stems chopped separately

1 teaspoon salt

500 ml (17 fl oz/2 cups) thin coconut milk (pages 8–9)

125 ml (4 fl oz/½ cup) thick coconut milk (pages 8–9)

To make the prawn stock, rinse the prawn heads and shells and drain well. Heat 1 tablespoon of the peanut oil in a saucepan and when very hot throw in the shells and heads. Stir-fry until they turn bright pink, then add 1 litre (34 fl oz/4 cups) hot water, bring to the boil, then reduce the heat to low and simmer until the liquid is reduced by half. Strain and reserve 500 ml (17 fl oz/2 cups) of the stock.

Heat the remaining oil in a large heavy-based saucepan over high heat. Add the onion and chilli and cook until the onion is soft and golden. Add the garlic and turmeric and stir-fry for 1 minute, then add the spinach stems and stir-fry for 3 minutes, add the salt, prawn stock and thin coconut milk, bring to the boil, then reduce the heat to low and simmer for 5 minutes. Add the spinach leaves and simmer for 3 minutes, then add the prawns and thick coconut milk. Bring back to the boil and boil for no more than 2–3 minutes. Serve straight away.

Soto Ayam
Chicken soup (spicy)

Serves: 6

1.5 kg (3 lb 5 oz) whole chicken

3 teaspoons salt

½ teaspoon whole black peppercorns

3–4 celery tops

1 large brown onion, sliced

2 tablespoons peanut oil

6 daun salam leaves (glossary) (optional)

2 garlic cloves, finely chopped

½ teaspoon finely grated fresh ginger

½ teaspoon dried shrimp paste

½ teaspoon ground turmeric

2 teaspoons ground coriander

1 teaspoon ground cumin

4 candlenuts or brazil nuts, finely grated

125 g (4½ oz) rice vermicelli (rice-stick) noodles

2 large potatoes, peeled, boiled and diced

lemon juice, to taste

8 spring onions (scallions), finely sliced, to garnish

2 hard-boiled eggs, peeled and finely chopped, to garnish

crumbled potato chips (crisps), to garnish

Joint the chicken (see page 13). Put the chicken pieces into a large saucepan with enough cold water to cover. Add the salt, peppercorns, celery tops and half of the onion. Bring to the boil, then reduce the heat to low, cover, and simmer for 30 minutes, or until the chicken is cooked through. Allow to cool, then strain and reserve the stock. Remove and discard the skin and bones and thinly slice the meat. Set aside.

Heat the peanut oil in the saucepan over medium heat. Add the daun salam leaves, if using, and the remaining onion and cook until the onion is golden. Add the garlic, ginger and shrimp paste, crushing the shrimp paste with the back of a spoon. Add the turmeric, coriander, cumin and candlenuts and stir-fry for a few seconds longer. Add the strained stock and bring back to the boil, then reduce the heat to low, cover, and simmer for 10 minutes.

Meanwhile, soak the rice vermicelli noodles according to the packet instructions, then drain and cut into short lengths. Add to the simmering soup, return to the boil, and cook for 1 minute. Add the chicken meat, potato and lemon juice and heat through. Pour into serving dishes and garnish with the spring onion and egg. Serve the potato chips in a separate bowl for sprinkling on individual servings.

Fish
and
Seafood

❀

Ikan Briani
Layered spiced fish and rice

Serves: 6

Fish savoury

750 g (1 lb 11 oz) firm white fish fillets
   or steaks

2 tablespoons lemon juice

2 teaspoons ground turmeric

oil for frying

2 onions, finely chopped

3 garlic cloves, crushed

1 teaspoon finely grated fresh ginger

3 teaspoons ground coriander

2 teaspoons ground cumin

1 large ripe tomato, peeled and chopped

60 ml (2 fl oz/¼ cup) thick coconut milk
   (pages 8–9)

Spiced rice

40 g (1½ oz) ghee

1 onion, thinly sliced

5 whole cardamom pods, bruised

4 whole cloves

1 small cinnamon stick

500 g (1 lb 2 oz/2½ cups) long-grain rice

1 litre (34 fl oz/4 cups) hot stock or water

2 teaspoons salt

Wipe the fish with damp paper towel. Cut each fish fillet into 2 or 3 pieces. Sprinkle lightly with the lemon juice and season with salt, pepper and 1½ teaspoons of the turmeric. Leave for 15 minutes.

Pour the oil into a large frying pan to a depth of 1 cm (½ in). Cook the fish over medium heat until lightly browned on both sides. Remove to a plate.

Pour all but 2 tablespoons of the oil from the pan and cook the onion, garlic and ginger until the onion is soft and translucent. Add the coriander, cumin and remaining turmeric and stir for 1 minute further. Add the tomato, about ¾ teaspoon salt and 125 ml (4 fl oz/½ cup) water, then cover and simmer until the tomato is cooked to a pulp. Add the coconut milk and simmer again, uncovered, until the mixture is smooth and thickened. Return the fish to the pan and spoon over the sauce, then continue to simmer for 3–4 minutes. Remove from the heat and keep warm.

To make the spiced rice, heat all but 1 teaspoon of the ghee in a frying pan over low heat. Add the onion and cook until golden. Add the whole spices and rice and stir-fry until the rice is well coated. Add the hot stock and salt, bring to the boil, then reduce the heat to low, cover, and simmer for 15 minutes. Remove from the heat and leave covered for 5 minutes. Uncover and lift out and discard the whole spices.

Preheat the oven to 160°C (320°F). Grease a 2 litre (68 fl oz/8 cup) capacity baking dish with the remaining ghee. Put one-third of the rice in an even layer in the prepared baking dish then pour over half of the fish savoury. Add another one-third of the rice in an even layer, then add the remaining fish savoury, and finish with a final layer of rice. Cover and cook for 25 minutes. Serve hot.

Note

If liked, this dish can be prepared a day ahead and refrigerated without baking, then heated in the oven before serving. Sprinkle the top with a little milk or water to prevent the rice grains drying out during baking, then cover with a lid or foil. Allow it to come to room temperature, then bake in the oven for 35–40 minutes.

Ikan Goreng Taucheo
Fried fish with salted soy beans

Serves: 4

500 g (1 lb 2 oz) fish steaks

oil for frying

2 onions, thinly sliced

2 garlic cloves, finely chopped

1 teaspoon finely grated fresh ginger

2 teaspoons salted soy bean paste (taucheo)

3 fresh red chillies, deseeded and sliced

1 teaspoon light soy sauce

lemon juice, to taste

Wipe the fish with damp paper towel. Pour the vegetable oil into a large frying pan to a depth of 1 cm (½ in). Cook the fish over medium heat until lightly golden on both sides. Drain on paper towel.

Pour off all but 2 tablespoons of the oil from the pan and cook the onion until soft and translucent. Add the garlic and ginger and cook until golden brown. Add the salted soy bean paste and stir-fry for 1 minute, then add the chilli, soy sauce and 190 ml (6½ fl oz/¾ cup) water. Allow to simmer until the sauce thickens slightly, then return the fish to the pan and cook for 5 minutes, turning once. Add the lemon juice to taste, and serve with white rice.

Ikan Kelapa
Spiced coconut fish

Serves: 4

500 g (1 lb 2 oz) firm white fish fillets

45 g (1½ oz/½ cup) desiccated (shredded) coconut

1 garlic clove

1 tablespoon finely grated fresh ginger

¼ teaspoon kencur (aromatic ginger) powder

1 teaspoon ground cumin

1 teaspoon ground coriander

1 teaspoon garam masala

1 teaspoon salt

1½ tablespoons lemon juice

1 tablespoon chopped fresh coriander (cilantro) leaves

four 20 cm (8 in) squares banana leaf

four 30 cm (12 in) squares foil

Wipe the fish with damp paper towel. Cut the fish into 10 cm (4 in) lengths.

Put the coconut, garlic, ginger, kencur powder, cumin, ground coriander, garam masala and salt into a food processor. Add 190 ml (6½ fl oz/¾ cup) hot water and process to a paste. Stir in the lemon juice and coriander leaves.

Place a square of banana leaf over a square of foil and place a quarter of the fish in the centre of each. Spoon 2–3 teaspoons of the coconut mixture over the top of each portion of fish, then close the leaves, followed by the foil, to make 4 parcels, sealing to enclose the fish. Steam for 15 minutes. Serve hot with rice and a vegetable side dish.

Gulai Ikan
Fish curry

Serves: 4–6

500 g (1 lb 2 oz) fish steaks

2 onions, roughly chopped

2 garlic cloves

2 teaspoons chopped fresh ginger

1 teaspoon Sambal ulek (page 104) or chilli powder

250 ml (8½ fl oz/1 cup) thin coconut milk (pages 8–9)

1 tablespoon ground coriander

1 teaspoon ground cumin

½ teaspoon ground fennel

½ teaspoon ground turmeric

2 strips thinly peeled lemon zest

6 curry leaves

2 tablespoons lemon juice

1 teaspoon salt

125 ml (4 fl oz/½ cup) thick coconut milk (pages 8–9)

Wipe the fish with damp paper towel. Cut the fish into serving pieces (see page 13).

Put the onion, garlic, ginger and sambal ulek into a food processor and process to a smooth paste, adding 1 tablespoon of the thin coconut milk if necessary. Scrape the blended mixture into a saucepan, wash out the food processor with the thin coconut milk and add to the pan with the ground spices, lemon zest and curry leaves. Bring to the boil, then reduce the heat to low and simmer for about 8 minutes. Add the fish, lemon juice and salt and simmer for 5 minutes. Add the thick coconut milk and stir until the curry reaches simmering point once more. Serve with rice.

Sambal Goreng Ikan
Fried fish sambal

Serves: 6

500 g (1 lb 2 oz) fresh sprats or small whitebait, about 5–7.5 cm (2–3 in) long

2 teaspoons tamarind pulp

1 onion, roughly chopped

2 candlenuts or brazil nuts

2 strips lemon zest

2 teaspoons chilli powder

1 teaspoon laos (dried galangal) powder

½ teaspoon dried shrimp paste

peanut oil for deep-frying

125 ml (4 fl oz/½ cup) thick coconut milk (pages 8–9)

5 daun salam leaves (glossary)

¾ teaspoon salt, or to taste

plain (all-purpose) flour for dusting

Wash the fish well. If using sprats, remove the heads and stomach bags. Rinse again in cold water and drain in a colander, then on paper towel. Set aside.

Soak the tamarind pulp in 80 ml (2½ fl oz/⅓ cup) hot water for 10 minutes. Squeeze to dissolve the pulp in the water, then strain, discarding the seeds and fibre.

Put the onion, candlenuts, lemon zest, chilli powder, laos powder and shrimp paste into a food processor and process to a smooth paste. It may be necessary to add a tablespoon or two of the tamarind liquid to enable the mixture to be drawn down on to the blades.

Heat 60 ml (2 fl oz/¼ cup) of the peanut oil in a wok or large heavy-based frying pan over low heat. Add the chilli mixture and stir until it darkens and the oil separates. Add the remaining tamarind liquid, coconut milk, daun salam leaves and salt and simmer until thick and oily. Remove from the heat and set aside.

Roll the fish in the flour to coat, shaking off any excess. Heat the peanut oil in a wok or large heavy-based saucepan over medium heat. When the oil is hot, deep-fry the fish, in batches, for 4–5 minutes, or until brown and crisp. Drain on paper towel.

To serve, add the fish to the warm spice mixture and stir to combine. Serve at once, while the fish is still crisp.

Acar Ikan
Vinegared fish

Serves: 6

500 g (1 lb 2 oz) fish steaks, such as tuna,
    kingfish or Spanish mackerel

juice of ½ lemon

2 small onions, 1 roughly chopped,
    1 thinly sliced

2 garlic cloves

1 teaspoon finely grated fresh ginger

3 candlenuts or brazil nuts

2 fresh red chillies, deseeded and chopped

1 tablespoon peanut oil

2 tablespoons vinegar

Wipe the fish with damp paper towel. Cut the fish steaks into serving pieces (see page 13). Rub with the lemon juice and season with a little salt. Set aside.

Put the chopped onion, garlic, ginger, candlenuts and chilli into a food processor with 2 tablespoons water and process to a smooth purée.

Heat the peanut oil in a wok or large heavy-based frying pan over medium heat. Cook the fish until golden on both sides. Remove to a plate.

Cook the sliced onion in the wok until golden brown. Add the chilli mixture and stir-fry for 3–4 minutes, or until the colour darkens. Add 80 ml (2½ fl oz/⅓ cup) water and some salt and simmer for 5 minutes, then add the vinegar and bring to the boil. Return the fish to the wok to heat through. Serve with white rice, vegetable dishes and sambals.

Ikan Kukus (Nonya)
Steamed fish (Straits Chinese style)

Serves: 4

4 dried shiitake mushrooms

500 g (1 lb 2 oz) firm white fish fillets

a few drops of sesame oil

3 tablespoons finely shredded Chinese
    preserved vegetables

1 fresh red chilli, deseeded and thinly sliced

2 teaspoons light soy sauce

2 spring onions (scallions), finely sliced

2 tablespoons fresh coriander (cilantro)
    leaves

1 lettuce leaf, shredded

Soak the dried mushrooms in 500 ml (17 fl oz/2 cups) hot water for 20–30 minutes, then drain, remove the stems and thinly slice the caps.

Wipe the fish with damp paper towel. Grease a heatproof dish with the sesame oil. Season the fish with salt and pepper and place in the dish. Scatter over the sliced mushroom, preserved vegetable, chilli and soy sauce, cover with foil and steam for 20 minutes. Garnish with the spring onion, coriander and lettuce. Serve with white rice.

Sambal Goreng Sotong
Squid sambal

Serves: 4–6

....

500 g (1 lb 2 oz) small squid

2 teaspoons tamarind pulp

2 onions, roughly chopped

2 garlic cloves

½ teaspoon dried shrimp paste

2 strips lemon zest

5 fresh red chillies or 1 teaspoon
    Sambal ulek (page 104)

1 tablespoon peanut oil

2 teaspoons chopped dark palm sugar
    (jaggery)

1–2 teaspoons paprika

Clean each squid, removing the ink sac and discarding the head. Rinse the tubes under cold running water and scrub to remove the skin. Drain well and slice into rings.

Soak the tamarind pulp in 80 ml (2½ fl oz/⅓ cup) hot water for 10 minutes. Squeeze to dissolve the pulp in the water, then strain, discarding the seeds and fibre.

Put the onion, garlic, shrimp paste, lemon zest and chilli into food processor and process to make a smooth paste, adding some of the peanut oil to help the mixture down onto the blades.

Heat the remaining oil in a wok or large heavy-based frying pan over medium heat. Add the chilli mixture and stir until it darkens and the oil separates. Add the tamarind liquid, palm sugar and paprika and stir in the squid. Cook for 5 minutes, stirring, until the squid is cooked and the mixture is thick and oily. Serve with rice.

Note

In Malaysia, a higher proportion of red chillies would be used to give colour to this dish, making paprika unnecessary.

Fish and Seafood ◆

Meat

❀

Kari Ayam Kelapa
Chicken curry with toasted coconut

Serves: 6

1.5 kg (3 lb 5 oz) whole chicken

4–6 fresh red chillies

45 g (1½ oz/½ cup) desiccated (shredded) coconut

500 ml (17 fl oz/2 cups) thick coconut milk (pages 8–9)

2 onions, roughly chopped

3 garlic cloves

1 teaspoon dried shrimp paste

1 teaspoon ground turmeric

1 tablespoon ground coriander

2 teaspoons ground cumin

1 stem lemongrass, sliced, or 2 strips lemon zest

60 ml (2 fl oz/¼ cup) peanut oil

2 teaspoons salt

8 daun salam leaves (glossary)

2 teaspoons laos (dried galangal) powder

Joint the chicken (see page 13) and cut into curry pieces.

Soak the chillies in hot water for 20 minutes. Drain well.

Put the coconut into a wok or large heavy-based frying pan over medium heat, stirring constantly, until it becomes a rich, dark brown. Remove to a plate.

Put the coconut into a food processor and process to a fine powder, then add 125 ml (4 fl oz/½ cup) of the coconut milk and process for 1 minute (in Asia fresh coconut would be roasted over coals and the nut meat then ground to a paste on a grinding stone). Remove the coconut mixture to a plate, and without washing the food processor, add the chillies, onion, garlic, shrimp paste, turmeric, coriander, cumin and lemongrass. Process to a purée, adding 1 tablespoon of the peanut oil, if needed.

Heat the remaining oil in a clean wok over low heat. Add the onion mixture, stirring constantly, until the moisture evaporates and the oil separates. Add the ground coconut, coconut milk, salt, daun salam leaves and laos powder and stir well. Add the chicken and stir gently, then simmer for 1 hour, or until the chicken is tender and cooked through. Serve with rice and other accompaniments.

Semur Ati
Spiced braised liver

Serves: 4

....

500 g (1 lb 2 oz) chicken livers or calves' livers

60 ml (2 fl oz/¼ cup) oil

1 onion, thinly sliced

2 garlic cloves, finely chopped

1 teaspoon finely grated fresh ginger

1½ teaspoons ground coriander

½ teaspoon ground cumin

½ teaspoon salt

¼ teaspoon freshly ground black pepper

2 tablespoons dark soy sauce

Thinly slice the liver – if using chicken livers remove the tubes and any discoloured spots and divide each one in half. Wash and drain on paper towel; set aside.

Heat the oil in a wok or large heavy-based frying pan over medium heat. Add the onion, garlic and ginger and cook, stirring frequently, for 5 minutes, or until golden. Add the liver in a single layer and sprinkle over the coriander, cumin, salt and pepper. Turn them and cook the other side for 2 minutes, then add the soy sauce and 80 ml (2½ fl oz/⅓ cup) water. Cover and simmer for about 5 minutes, depending on the thickness of the slices; be careful to not overcook, the liver should lose its pinkness inside but not be allowed to get hard and dry. Serve immediately.

Ayam Lemak
Chicken with spicy coconut milk gravy

Serves: 6

....

1.5 kg (3 lb 5 oz) whole chicken

2½ teaspoons finely grated fresh ginger

2 onions, chopped

3 stems lemongrass, white part only, sliced or finely grated zest of 1 lemon

6 fresh red chillies, deseeded and chopped, or 2 teaspoons Sambal ulek (page 104)

1 teaspoon ground turmeric

60 ml (2 fl oz/¼ cup) oil

750 ml (25½ fl oz/3 cups) thick coconut milk (pages 8–9)

1 pandanus leaf or 3 fresh basil leaves

2 teaspoons salt

Joint the chicken (see page 13) and cut into serving pieces.

Pound the ginger, onion, lemongrass and chilli using a mortar and pestle, or grind in an electric spice grinder with a little oil until a paste forms.

Rub the turmeric over the chicken pieces to coat.

Heat the oil in a wok or large heavy-based saucepan over low heat. Add the chilli mixture and stir constantly for 15 minutes, or until soft and golden. Add the chicken and fry for a further 10 minutes, then add the coconut milk, pandanus leaf and salt and simmer until the chicken is tender. Serve with white rice.

Gulai Ayam Rebong
Chicken and bamboo shoot curry

Serves: 6–8

1.5 kg (3 lb 5 oz) whole chicken

2 onions, finely chopped

80 ml (2½ fl oz/⅓ cup) coconut or
    peanut oil

1½ tablespoons ground coriander

1 teaspoon dried shrimp paste

1 teaspoon laos (dried galangal) powder

1 teaspoon chilli powder

2 teaspoons salt

500 ml (17 fl oz/2 cups) thin coconut milk
    (pages 8–9)

310 g (11 oz/1¼ cups) tinned, drained
    bamboo shoots, thinly sliced

250 ml (8½ fl oz/1 cup) thick coconut milk
    (page 8–9)

Joint the chicken (see page 13) and cut into curry pieces.

Heat the coconut oil in a large heavy-based saucepan over medium heat. Add the onion and cook until soft and golden. Add the coriander, shrimp paste, laos powder, chilli powder and salt, and cook for 3 minutes, stirring constantly, until the spices are brown. Add the chicken and stir until well coated in the spices, then add the thin coconut milk and simmer for 20–25 minutes.

Add the bamboo shoots to the pan and continue simmering for a further 20 minutes, or until the chicken is tender. Add the thick coconut milk and simmer, stirring gently until the oil starts to separate and rise to the surface. Taste and add salt if necessary. Serve with rice, vegetables and sambal.

Rendang Ayam
Chicken in coconut milk

Serves: 6

1.5 kg (3 lb 5 oz) whole chicken

2 onions, roughly chopped

4 garlic cloves, sliced

2 teaspoons finely chopped fresh ginger

2 stems lemongrass, white part only, sliced, or 4 strips lemon zest

4 fresh red chillies, deseeded and chopped

500 ml (17 fl oz/2 cups) coconut milk (pages 8–9)

2 slices fresh galangal or 1 teaspoon laos (dried galangal) powder

1 teaspoon ground coriander

1 teaspoon ground turmeric

4 daun salam leaves (glossary)

½ teaspoon freshly ground black pepper

1½ teaspoons salt

Joint the chicken (see page 13) and cut into curry pieces.

Put the onion, garlic, ginger, lemongrass and chilli into a food processor with 125 ml (4 fl oz/½ cup) of the coconut milk and process to a smooth purée.

Put the chilli mixture into a large saucepan with the remaining coconut milk, laos powder, coriander, turmeric, daun salam leaves, pepper and salt. Bring slowly to the boil, stirring occasionally – do not cover the pan or the coconut milk will curdle. Add the chicken, bring back to the boil, then reduce the heat to low and simmer until the chicken is tender. Serve with white rice.

Note

This dish should continue cooking until the sauce has almost been absorbed – try to get a boiling fowl, or by the time the sauce has reduced the flesh will be falling off the bones. The more readily available roasting chicken can be served when it is cooked through and impregnated with the flavours of the sauce, even though it has not completely absorbed them.

Gulai Ayam
Whole chicken curry

Serves: 6–8

You really need a tough boiling chicken for this recipe, because the longer the cooking time, the better the flavour. If using a roasting chicken, shorten the cooking time so that the chicken doesn't fall apart, and reduce the sauce as described at the end of the recipe.

2 kg (4 lb 6 oz) whole chicken

750 ml–1 litre (25½–34 fl oz/3–4 cups) thin coconut milk (pages 8–9)

3 teaspoons chilli powder, or to taste

2 teaspoons ground cumin

½ teaspoon ground turmeric

¼ teaspoon fenugreek seeds

2 teaspoons salt

1 onion, thinly sliced

3 garlic cloves, finely chopped

2 teaspoons finely chopped fresh ginger

1 stem lemongrass or 2 strips lemon zest

1 small cinnamon stick

1 pandanus leaf (optional)

1½ teaspoons ground fennel

2 tablespoons lemon juice

20 g (¾ oz) ghee

Truss the chicken as for roasting and put it into a large saucepan with enough coconut milk to come two-thirds of the way up the bird. Add all the remaining ingredients, except the fennel, lemon juice and ghee. Bring to the boil, then reduce the heat to low and simmer for 30 minutes. Add the fennel and lemon juice, turn the bird over, and continue simmering until the chicken is tender, adding more hot water or coconut milk if the liquid cooks away.

Pour the sauce into a bowl, leaving the bird in the pan. Add the ghee to the pan and fry the bird, turning it on all sides, until golden brown all over.

Remove the chicken from the pan after browning, pour the sauce back into the pan to reduce and once thickened return the chicken to heat through. Add more salt and lemon juice, to taste. Serve with rice and other curries.

Shami Kebab
Mutton and lentil rissoles

Serves: 4

125 g (4½ oz/½ cup) red lentils or
  yellow split peas

250 g (9 oz) lean minced (ground) mutton,
  lamb or beef

2 onions, finely chopped

¼ teaspoon ground cinnamon

¼ teaspoon ground cardamom

⅛ teaspoon ground cloves

1 teaspoon salt

½ teaspoon freshly ground black pepper

1 egg, beaten

2 tablespoons finely chopped fresh mint

oil for frying

Wash the lentils or split peas well, then drain. Put the lentils into a saucepan with 500 ml (17 fl oz/2 cups) water and bring to the boil. Add the minced meat and onion, and cook over medium–low heat, stirring occasionally, until the lentils are cooked – stir as the mixture starts to dry and continue cooking until the liquid is completely absorbed.

Turn the mixture into a bowl and when cool enough to handle, use your hands to mix in the cinnamon, cardamom, cloves, salt, pepper, egg and fresh mint. Mix thoroughly, then shape into about 8 flat round rissoles.

Heat the oil in a large heavy-based frying pan and cook the rissoles until golden brown on both sides. Drain and serve hot.

Satay Daging
Malay beef satay

Serves: 6

This is a surprisingly flavoursome marinade – despite the absence of garlic, onion and ginger. Serve hot off the barbecue, accompanied by *ketupat* and chilli peanut sauce.

750 g (1 lb 11 oz) rump steak

2 teaspoons ground turmeric

2 teaspoons ground cumin

2 teaspoons ground fennel

finely grated zest of 1 lemon

1½ teaspoons salt

1 tablespoon sugar

80 ml (2½ fl oz/⅓ cup) thick coconut milk
(pages 8–9)

Soak bamboo skewers in cold water to prevent them from burning during cooking.

Cut the beef into 2 cm (¾ in) cubes, trimming off most of the fat, leaving a thin layer on some of the cubes. Cut the trimmed fat into thin squares and reserve.

Combine the turmeric, cumin, fennel, lemon zest, salt, sugar and coconut milk in a bowl and stir to dissolve the sugar. Add the beef and toss well to coat. Leave to marinate for at least 1 hour, or overnight in the refrigerator – the longer it marinates the more flavoursome it will be.

Thread about 5 pieces of meat onto each skewer. Use the squares of fat where necessary, especially where the meat is very lean, as this will help to keep the meat tender during cooking. Grill over hot coals or under a preheated grill (broiler) until the beef is well cooked and crisp.

Gulai Kambing
Spicy mutton curry

Serves: 6

60 g (2 oz/⅔ cup) desiccated (shredded)
  coconut

2 teaspoons tamarind pulp

2 large onions, roughly chopped

4 garlic cloves

1 tablespoon roughly chopped fresh ginger

2 teaspoons ground coriander

1 teaspoon ground cumin

1 teaspoon ground turmeric

½ teaspoon ground cinnamon

½ teaspoon ground fennel

½ teaspoon freshly grated nutmeg

½ teaspoon freshly ground black pepper

¼ teaspoon ground cloves

¼ teaspoon ground cardamom

4 candlenuts or brazil nuts

4–8 dried red chillies, or to taste

1 stem lemongrass or 1 teaspoon finely
  grated lemon zest

2 tablespoons peanut oil

750 g (1 lb 11 oz) mutton, cut into
  small cubes

2 ripe tomatoes, chopped

375 ml (12½ fl oz/1½ cups) coconut milk
  (pages 8–9)

1½ teaspoons salt

Put the coconut in a dry frying pan over medium–low heat and cook for 4–5 minutes, or until it is a rich golden brown. Remove to a plate to cool.

Soak the tamarind pulp in 60 ml (2 fl oz/¼ cup) hot water for 10 minutes. Squeeze to dissolve the pulp in the water, then strain, discarding the seeds and fibre. Put into a food processor with the onion and process to make a smooth, thick paste. Add the garlic and ginger and process to combine, then add the ground spices, candlenuts, dried chillies and toasted coconut and process until smooth and well combined. If lemon zest is being used it can be processed too, but if lemongrass is available add it later.

Heat the peanut oil in a large heavy-based saucepan over low heat. Add the coconut mixture and cook for 5 minutes, stirring frequently at the beginning and constantly at the end. Add the meat and cook for 3 minutes, stirring well so that each piece is coated with the spices. Add the tomato and cook for a further 3 minutes, then add the coconut milk, salt and lemongrass, if using, and bring slowly to the boil. Reduce the heat to low and simmer for 1½–2 hours, or until the meat is tender, stirring occasionally. Serve with white rice.

Vegetables and Accompaniments

❖

Sayur Masak Lemak
Vegetable curry

Serves: 6 as an accompaniment

1 onion, thinly sliced

1 garlic clove, finely chopped

2 fresh red or green chillies, deseeded
  and sliced

½ teaspoon dried shrimp paste

½ teaspoon ground turmeric

250 ml (8½ fl oz/1 cup) thin coconut milk
  (pages 8–9)

1 large potato, peeled and diced

225 g (8 oz/3 cups) shredded white cabbage

1 teaspoon salt

250 ml (8½ fl oz/1 cup) thick coconut milk
  (pages 8–9)

lemon juice, to taste

Put the onion, garlic, chilli, dried shrimp paste, turmeric and thin coconut milk into a saucepan and bring to simmering point. Add the potato and cook for 10 minutes, or until the potato is half cooked.

Add the cabbage and salt to the pan and cook for 3 minutes, then add the thick coconut milk and stir gently until the cabbage is tender and the potato is cooked through. Remove from the heat and add the lemon juice to taste. Serve hot.

Taukwa Dan Taugeh
Tofu and bean sprouts

Serves: 6

380 g (13½ oz) firm tofu

2 tablespoons oil

2 garlic cloves, crushed

180 g (6½ oz/2 cups) fresh bean sprouts,
  trimmed

soy sauce, to taste

Cut the tofu into thick slices.

Heat the oil in a wok or large heavy-based saucepan over low heat. Add the garlic and cook until golden, then add the tofu and bean sprouts and stir-fry for 3–4 minutes, or until heated through. Add the soy sauce to taste and season with the salt and freshly ground black pepper. Serve immediately.

Taukwa Taucheo
Tofu in salted soy bean paste

Serves: 6

2 tablespoons peanut oil

2 garlic cloves, finely chopped

3 fresh red chillies, deseeded and finely chopped

2 teaspoons salted soy bean paste (taucheo)

250 g (9 oz) raw prawns (shrimp), peeled and deveined or 85 g (3 oz/½ cup) crabmeat

380 g (13½ oz) firm tofu, cut into small cubes

1 tablespoon light soy sauce

2 tablespoons chopped celery leaves

2 tablespoons chopped spring onions (scallions)

Heat the peanut oil in a wok or large heavy-based frying pan over low heat. Add the garlic and chilli and cook until the garlic starts to brown, then add the salted soy bean paste and stir-fry for 1 minute.

Add the prawns to the wok and stir-fry until cooked through, then add the tofu, soy sauce and 60 ml (2 fl oz/¼ cup) water and cook until the liquid is absorbed. Season with salt, to taste. Remove from the heat, stir in the celery leaves and spring onion and serve hot.

Sambal Kelapa
Coconut sambal

Serves: 6

½ teaspoon dried shrimp paste

60 g (2 oz/1 cup) fresh grated coconut or 90 g (3 oz/1 cup) desiccated (shredded) coconut moistened in 2 tablespoons hot water

1 teaspoon salt

½–1 teaspoon chilli powder or 1 fresh red chilli, deseeded and chopped

2 tablespoons finely chopped onion

1 small garlic clove, crushed

juice of ½ lemon

Wrap the shrimp paste in a piece of foil and roast under a preheated grill (broiler) for 5 minutes, turning halfway through the cooking time. Unwrap and place in a bowl with the remaining ingredients, using your hands to combine thoroughly. Serve as an accompaniment to rice and curries.

Sambal Goreng Kembang
Chilli-fried cauliflower

Serves: 6

....

60 ml (2 fl oz/¼ cup) peanut oil

4 fresh red chillies, deseeded and finely
   chopped, or 2 teaspoons Sambal ulek
   (page 104)

1 large onion, finely chopped

2 garlic cloves, finely chopped

1 teaspoon dried shrimp paste

1 teaspoon salt

500 g (1 lb 2 oz) cauliflower, broken into
   small florets

Heat the peanut oil in a wok or frying pan over low heat. Add the chilli, onion and garlic and cook until the onion is soft and golden. Add the dried shrimp paste, crush with the back of a spoon and stir-fry for 1 minute, then add the salt and cauliflower and toss constantly until the cauliflower is thoroughly mixed and coated with the spices. Sprinkle with 2 tablespoons hot water, cover, and cook for 10 minutes, or until tender. Serve hot.

Acar Kuning
Vegetable pickle

Makes: 3 cups

2 tablespoons peanut oil

2 garlic cloves, finely grated

2 teaspoons finely grated fresh ginger

3 candlenuts or brazil nuts, grated

1 teaspoon ground turmeric

125 ml (4 fl oz/½ cup) white vinegar

2 teaspoons sugar

1 teaspoon salt

90 g (3 oz/1 cup) julienne carrots

125 g (4½ oz/1 cup) sliced green beans

10 fresh red and green chillies, stems removed

1 green cucumber, peeled, deseeded and julienned

125 g (4½ oz/1 cup) cauliflower florets

Heat the peanut oil in a saucepan over low heat. Add the garlic and ginger and cook for 1 minute, then add the grated candlenuts and turmeric and cook for a few seconds longer. Add the vinegar, sugar, salt and 125 ml (4 fl oz/½ cup) water and bring to the boil, then add the carrot, beans, chilli and cauliflower. Bring back to the boil and boil for 3 minutes, then add the cucumber and boil for 1 minute longer.

Turn into an earthenware or glass bowl and allow to cool. Use immediately or store in sterilised airtight jars in the refrigerator for up to 2 weeks.

Roti Jala
Lacy pancakes

Makes: about 12 pancakes

These pancakes are served with Spicy mutton curry (page 146) or other rich, dry curries and form a substantial snack that is almost a meal.

2 eggs

685 ml (23 fl oz/2¾ cups) thin coconut milk (pages 8–9) or fresh milk

300 g (10½ oz/2 cups) plain (all-purpose) flour, sifted

½ teaspoon salt

2 tablespoons oil

Beat together the eggs and coconut milk until well combined.

Put the flour and salt into a large bowl and steadily add the egg mixture, stirring constantly with a wooden spoon. Do not add liquid too slowly at first or it will be difficult to get rid of the lumps. When all the liquid has been added, beat until the batter is smooth.

Heat a little of the oil in a heavy-based omelette pan or pancake pan and pour in some of the batter, moving the ladle back and forth so that the pancake will have a perforated appearance. Cook until set and pale golden underneath, then turn and cook the other side until cooked through. Remove to a plate and keep warm. Repeat with the remaining batter to make 12 pancakes in total. If the batter thickens on standing, add a little water and stir well to combine before cooking.

Saus Kacang
Chilli and peanut sauce

Makes: 2 cups

oil for deep-frying

160 g (5½ oz/1 cup) raw peanuts

10 large dried red chillies

1 teaspoon tamarind pulp

1 onion, roughly chopped

6 garlic cloves, peeled

½ teaspoon dried shrimp paste

60 ml (2 fl oz/¼ cup) coconut oil or
   peanut oil

1 teaspoon salt

250 ml (8½ fl oz/1 cup) thick coconut milk
   (pages 8–9)

1 tablespoon chopped dark palm sugar
   (jaggery)

Heat the oil in a wok or large heavy-based saucepan over medium heat. When the oil is hot, deep-fry the peanuts until just golden, then remove them using a slotted spoon and drain on paper towel. The peanuts will continue to cook in their own heat, so don't leave them in the oil until they are brown or they will be overdone and bitter. Rub off the skins and pound, crush or process until they are coarsely ground – they should be crisp and have lots of crunchy bits, not worked to a smooth paste.

Put the dry chillies in a bowl with 500 ml (17 fl oz/2 cups) hot water. Leave to soak for 20 minutes. Drain and reserve 2 tablespoons of the soaking liquid. Soak the tamarind pulp in 1 tablespoon hot water for 10 minutes. Squeeze to dissolve the pulp in the water, then strain, discarding the seeds and fibre

Put the soaked chillies and reserved soaking liquid into a food processor with the onion, garlic and dried shrimp paste and process to make a smooth paste.

Heat the coconut oil in a wok or large heavy-based frying pan over medium heat. Add the chilli mixture and stir-fry until it darkens. Remove from the heat and stir in the tamarind liquid, salt, coconut milk and palm sugar and transfer to a bowl to cool. When the sauce has cooled stir in the peanuts so they retain their crunchiness. Serve hot with Malay beef satay (page 144) and Compressed rice cakes (page 121). Garnish with sliced cucumber – it is ideal to cool the heat of the sauce.

Sweets
and
Desserts

❀

Serikaya Dengan Agar-Agar
Coconut milk jelly

Serves: 6–8

3 cardamom pods, bruised

1 small cinnamon stick

5 teaspoons agar-agar powder

450 g (1 lb/2½ cups) finely chopped dark palm sugar (jaggery)

500 ml (17 fl oz/2 cups) thick coconut milk (pages 8–9)

1 pinch of salt

ground cinnamon, to garnish

Put the cardamom pods, cinnamon and 1.5 litres (51 fl oz/ 6 cups) water into a saucepan over medium–high heat. Sprinkle the agar-agar powder evenly over the surface of the water to prevent it from forming lumps. Bring to the boil, add the palm sugar, then reduce the heat to low and simmer for 10 minutes, stirring occasionally, until the agar-agar and sugar have dissolved.

Add the coconut milk and salt to the pan and stir constantly until it just starts to simmer – do not boil or it may curdle. Strain through a fine sieve and pour into 6 or 8 moulds or small bowls. Allow to cool to room temperature, then refrigerate to set and serve chilled with a light dusting of cinnamon to garnish.

Gula Melaka
Sago pudding

Serves: 6–8

'Gula melaka' means palm sugar, but it is so integral a part of the recipe that this popular dessert has become known by the same name. Sago pudding takes on a new dimension when prepared this way. Palm sugar (jaggery) is sometimes sold under the name of coconut sugar or coconut preserves – a solid cylinder of concentrated sweetness derived from the sap of coconut or other varieties of palm. If you have a choice of light or dark palm sugar, choose the dark as the colour and flavour is more authentic. If dark palm sugar is difficult to find, substitute an equivalent amount of dark brown sugar and maple syrup – for each 180 g (6½ oz/1 cup) of sugar add 125 ml (4 fl oz/½ cup) maple syrup.

390 g (14 oz/2 cups) sago

1 small cinnamon stick (optional)

340 ml (11½ fl oz/1⅓ cups) coconut milk (pages 8–9)

1 pinch of salt

240 g (8½ oz/1⅓ cup) finely chopped dark palm sugar (jaggery)

2 pandanus leaves

Put 2–2.5 litres (68–85 fl oz/8–10 cups) water in a large saucepan and bring to the boil, then slowly pour in the sago and add the cinnamon stick, if using. Let it boil for 5–7 minutes, then turn off the heat, cover, and leave to finish cooking off the heat for 10 minutes – when done, the grains will be clear. Run cold water into the pan, stir well, then drain in a sieve, shaking the sieve so the water runs off and discarding the cinnamon.

Turn the sago into a bowl, stir in 2 tablespoons of the coconut milk and the salt. Divide among 6 or 8 moulds or small bowls and refrigerate until set.

Make a sugar syrup by putting the palm sugar and 125 ml (4 fl oz/½ cup) water in a saucepan with the pandanus leaves and stir over medium heat until the sugar has dissolved. Strain through a fine sieve, then allow to cool and refrigerate until chilled.

To serve, turn the puddings out of their moulds into serving dishes and serve with the chilled syrup and remaining coconut milk at room temperature, in separate pitchers.

Singapore

Singapore is a gourmet's dream come true. Any kind of food you wish to eat, Eastern or Western, is available at its best in this cosmopolitan city. I have eaten some of the best Chinese meals of my life in Singapore, at exclusive restaurants and at street stalls, not to mention Malay, Indian and Japanese food that made me look forward with eagerness to future visits.

But the most interesting food, because it is peculiar to the regions where the Chinese settled and intermarried with the locals, is the Nonya (or Nyonya) style of food – a mixture of Chinese ingredients and Malay spices, cooked in a way that is a perfect mingling of the two cultures. 'Peranakan' is the term given to Chinese people born in the British-run Straits Settlements of Singapore, Malacca and Penang; the women known as 'Nonyas', the men 'Babas'.

There is conjecture as to when the Nonya or Peranakan culture began. Some say as early as 1459, when a Chinese Princess was given to the ruling Sultan of Malacca as a means of strengthening ties between the nations following a visit to that trading port by Chinese Admiral Cheng Ho. Her entourage followed her example and married locals. In the nineteenth century, enterprising Peranakan traders from Malacca were lured by the newer ports of Penang and Singapore, followed by an influx of Chinese labour, swelling the Nonya population and establishing a strong presence of Nonya traditions in those areas. The result was a singular and quite distinctive style of cooking that is preserved today not only in Singapore, but also Malacca, Penang and to a lesser extent Java; a cuisine that the Peranakan are proud of and cannot live without.

In 1979 I had the chance to meet and speak with the late Mrs Lee Chin Koon, author of *Nonya Cuisine*, the most comprehensive volume available on Nonya cooking at that time and a keen practical cook with 50 years' experience. Her aim in teaching, cooking and writing her recipes was to ensure that Nonya cooking was kept alive – as the younger generation became less interested in the domestic arts and became more career conscious. Their entertaining was done in restaurants and with the increased tempo of life and the new freedom Eastern women enjoyed, young wives no longer spent hours in the kitchen with the older women of the household, watching, helping and learning. Apart from her accomplishments in the culinary field, the alert and energetic seventy year old was the mother of Singapore's popular and powerful Prime Minister at that time, Lee Kuan Yew, and was affectionately referred to as 'Mama Lee'.

'To us, our Nonya food is very special and we prefer to eat it to any other type of food. It is totally different from Chinese food, though we do use some Chinese ingredients, like pork, which the Malays, who are Muslims, are forbidden to touch or eat,' writes Mrs Lee. 'Ingredients found in Malay, Indonesian and Chinese kitchens can be found in our kitchens, however not all of our ingredients can be found in other typical Chinese kitchens.'

Nonya recipes are often hot and spicy. As well as using Chinese ingredients in some dishes, they add herbs and spices that are never used in traditional Chinese food. Many recipes are based on a *rempah*, a paste of various spices including hot chillies, spring onions (scallions), lemongrass, candlenuts, lengkuas (galangal), turmeric and blacan pounded to just the right degree with a stone mortar and pestle. The pounding itself is an art that must be mastered – too little and the paste will not be smooth enough, too much and it will become too liquid.

I understood perfectly what Mama Lee meant when she said the recipes in her book are six generations old but that the book itself represents seven years of work, merely to translate the *agak*, or estimated measures, into cups and spoons, precise weights and measures. In writing down Asian recipes I have had this problem myself.

Even with recipes that have been in the family for years, one finds they are done by instinct and learned almost by a process of osmosis. Young cooks learn from their mothers, grandmothers, aunts and after marriage from the all-powerful mother-in-law. There are no written recipes or precise measures. Experienced cooks know just how much of this or that ingredient to use and the amount can vary depending on how strong or fresh the ginger or garlic is, how hot the chillies, how large or how small the spring onions or stems of lemongrass. When it comes to passing on the recipes, especially to cooks who may be making a dish for the first time and do not know how hot or sour or salty it should be, it requires the utmost discipline to do every recipe over again, measuring by standard cups and spoons, trying to even out all the variables and write down the method in painstaking detail.

Mrs Lee's attitude towards sharing recipes was a refreshing change from the unwillingness that characterises many Asian women who have built themselves a reputation as good cooks and who guard their secrets jealously. A request to divulge a recipe may be met with a firm refusal; or a vital ingredient or step in preparation may be left out so that attempts to duplicate a dish will not be successful. Mrs Lee decried this attitude and wished only that good Nonya cooking should survive. 'A good recipe is meant to be shared,' she stated firmly, and I could not agree more.

I cannot remember every meal I have eaten in the garden city of Singapore, but some are outstanding and cannot be forgotten. There was the Kashmir style food at the Omar Khayyam, owned and run by Mr Wadhu Sakhrani, a gracious and most knowledgeable host. The exquisite decor, the original paintings done by an Indian artist (which are enlargements of very old miniatures) and the small alcoves in the walls, each one holding a simple oil lamp, set the mood for the meal to come. And when it came it was perfect in every detail. I have never eaten better Indian food, in or out of India. Typical of Kashmiri food, there were no mind-blowing hot tastes. Instead, there were exquisite fragrances and delicate spicing.

As Mr Sakhrani's guest I was invited to sample a much larger variety of dishes than could normally be consumed at a single meal. Tandoori chicken rubbed with a spice marinade and cooked in a fiercely hot clay oven buried in the earth becomes tender, golden brown and crisp, with a flavour that defies description; Kashmiri prawn (shrimp) curry, richly red but not hot; kofta of finely minced (ground) tender lamb, spiced and sauced; chicken livers cooked in spices, onions, herbs and ginger; chicken simmered in butter with herbs and tomatoes. Then a raita that was smooth, rich and creamy, given a special, extravagant touch with pistachio nuts; Persian pilau cooked with saffron, orange zest and almonds; *biriani nentara*, a vegetable and rice preparation; *Khayyam naan*, one of the large flatbreads so popular in India. And, to finish the feast, koulfi – the ice cream of Kashmir that bears no resemblance to the fluffy, gelatine-boosted ice creams of the West; and *ras malai*, queen of Indian desserts, featuring homemade cream cheese, rose and cardamom flavourings and rich clotted cream.

Another meal to remember was a superb Sichuan-style banquet at the Golden Phoenix restaurant in the Hotel Equatorial, which was reputedly the best place to eat Sichuan food. Cold hors d'oeuvre, including marinated duck and strips of jellyfish, deep-fried prawns and chillies, stir-fried chicken and vegetables and Sichuan soup – sour, slightly hot, laden with shredded pork, prawns, tofu and shiitake mushrooms so that a small bowl of it was rich and filling. The Sichuan pancake served for dessert was a totally new experience – a very thin crepe filled with sweet bean paste and folded over to enclose it, then fried until golden and crisp on the outside. Toasted sesame seeds clung to the batter and even when folded it filled a large Chinese dish, so I could not help but wonder at how large the pancake must have been at first. It was brought to the table neatly cut into bite-sized strips but left in the original shape.

While these meals were superbly presented and cooked by experts, there was an element of fun and informality added when we dined at the Orchard Road Car Park, which is sadly no more. By day it was a car park, but at night it turned into one of those outdoor eateries for which Singapore was famous. No snowy white cloths or elegant decor here. Instead, you could wander around watching each chef cooking his speciality and decide which to order. You could partake of a dozen different noodle dishes; curries and roti in Indian or Malay style; fried rice, chilli crabs, satay and sauces, *poh pia* – in fact just about any Chinese, Indian, Indonesian or Malay food you care to name.

And you'd top it off with one of the local sweets or with a glass of freshly pressed juice. Orange and sugar cane vie for top place and it was sugar cane juice, frothy and pale green and just pressed, that I chose. It is one of the most refreshing drinks – not too sweet and very clean tasting. While it lacks the tang of lime or orange it has a delicacy of flavour I have not met in any other drink. Tinned sugar cane juice is a poor substitute. It has none of the fresh flavour or refreshing quality, and if not for the label on the tin it would be hard to identify with the fresh product, so wait until you can taste the real thing or pass it up.

Serving and eating a Nonya meal

While Singapore is predominantly Chinese, I am representing Nonya cooking in this chapter, for this originated here and is synonymous with Singapore. It is, as with most Asian meals, all served at one time. Rice or noodles, curries, sambal, soup and vegetable dishes are placed on the table and each person makes their own choice.

Dinner plates are used for eating. While the traditional way is to mix and eat the spicy food with the fingers, modern manners favour the use of spoon and fork. This type of food is called *lauk pering*, or food served on a plate. When soup dishes such as laksa or *meehoon* are on the menu they are served in Chinese-style bowls. To finish the meal, sweets made of glutinous rice and coconut milk are popular. Wine is not served with this kind of food, and instead of Chinese tea most Nonyas prefer to drink Malay coffee.

Utensils

The traditional kitchen with its wood fire is almost a thing of the past. In modern high-rise housing developments that have taken the place of the *kampung* (clusters of little shacks huddled together in a common garden) modern gas stoves are used. Even where *kampung* persist, the tin or thatched roof shacks have been replaced with neat wooden houses and the kitchens too have been modernised.

For curry cooking the traditional vessel is the clay *chatty* so popular in Southeast Asia. Discerning cooks treasure their special clay pots as much as a French cook holds sacred an omelette pan.

For Chinese or Nonya-style cooking a wok or *kuali* is best; you'll also need a sharp Chinese chopper and heavy wooden chopping board. A heavy mortar and pestle is invaluable for pounding spices and most cooks cherish their grinding stones, but a powerful electric blender can replace these two essentials in a Western kitchen. A coconut grater is also essential in an Asian kitchen, but nowadays cooks buy fresh grated coconut at the market. Again, a food processor or blender can be used for making coconut milk (pages 8–9).

Good-quality saucepans, a deep frying pan, wooden spoons and the usual frying spoons found in any reasonably well-equipped kitchen will cope with the recipes in this chapter. For deep-frying, a slotted spoon and a wire or mesh skimmer will be invaluable.

Your Singapore shelf

This is a list of spices, sauces, sambals and other flavourings which are often used in Nonya cooking and good to have on hand to make the recipes in this chapter.

black pepper, freshly ground	galangal, in brine and fresh
candlenuts or brazil nuts	hoisin sauce
chilli powder	laos (dried galangal) powder
chilli sauce	oyster sauce
chillies, dried red	peanut oil
Chinese barbecue (char siu) sauce	peanuts, unsalted
Chinese five-spice	rice vermicelli (rice-stick) noodles
Chinese rice wine or dry sherry	salted black beans, tinned
cinnamon, ground	salted soy bean paste (taucheo)
coconut milk and cream (pages 8–9)	sesame oil
coconut, desiccated (shredded)	sesame seeds
coriander, ground	shiitake mushrooms, dried
cornflour (cornstarch)	soy sauce, light and dark
cumin, ground	tamarind pulp
dried shrimp paste	turmeric, ground
egg noodles	wood ear fungus, dried
fennel, ground	

Rice,
Noodles
and Snacks

Nasi Lemak
Coconut rice

Serves: 4–5

Though traditional nasi lemak is simply flavoured with salt and coconut milk, some cooks like to enhance the flavour with pandanus. Tie two or three lengths of pandanus leaf into a knot to fit easily in the pan and so they are easy to remove. Add it to the liquid in which the rice will be cooked and remove after the rice is cooked.

500 g (1 lb 2 oz/2½ cups) long-grain rice

310 ml (10½ fl oz/1¼ cups) coconut milk (pages 8–9)

2½ teaspoons salt

Variation

You can mix 400 ml (13½ fl oz) coconut milk and 350 ml (12 fl oz) water in a saucepan with 2 teaspoons salt and bring it to the boil. Add 400 g (14 oz/2 cups) long-grain rice, stir, reduce the heat to low, and cook uncovered until the surface of the rice is dotted with little holes. Cover and cook for 7 minutes, then allow to rest without lifting the lid for another 5 minutes before serving. If you would like a less rich result, increase the water and decrease the coconut milk. As long as the total liquid content is 750 ml (25½ fl oz/3 cups) the consistency will be correct for that amount of rice.

Soak the rice in water overnight. Drain well, then spread the rice in the top basin of a steamer and steam over rapidly boiling water for 30 minutes. Halfway through steaming, stir the rice so that it cooks evenly.

Put the coconut milk and salt in a large saucepan with a tight-fitting lid over medium heat, stirring often, but do not boil. Add the steamed rice to the coconut milk, stir well, cover, then remove from the heat and let stand for a further 30 minutes, or until the milk is completely absorbed.

Spread the rice in the top of the steamer once more and steam over rapidly boiling water for a further 30 minutes, starting on high heat and gradually reducing the heat until just simmering, until the rice is tender and all the liquid has been absorbed. Serve the coconut rice hot with meat, poultry, fish or vegetable dishes, both mild and hot.

Chee Cheong Fun
Fresh rice noodle snack

Serves: 2–3

500 g (1 lb 2 oz) fresh rice noodles

1 tablespoon Chinese barbecue (char siu) sauce

1 tablespoon light soy sauce

1 teaspoon sesame oil

1 teaspoon sweet chilli sauce

1 tablespoon lightly toasted sesame seeds

Cut the rice noodles into thin strips. Place into a bowl and pour boiling water over them, cover and leave to soak for 5 minutes. Alternatively, put the sliced noodles in a colander and steam over a saucepan of boiling water for a few minutes until heated through. Drain well and put the noodles into a serving bowl. Add the remaining ingredients and toss lightly to combine.

Fresh Noodles, Fried

Serves: 4–6

3 rashers (slices) bacon or cooked pork, trimmed and thinly sliced

60 ml (2 fl oz/¼ cup) oil

250 g (9 oz) lean beef steak, thinly sliced

250 g (9 oz) raw small prawns (shrimp), peeled and deveined

2 teaspoons salted soy bean paste (taucheo)

4 garlic cloves, crushed

1 teaspoon finely grated fresh ginger

150 g (5½ oz/2 cups) shredded Chinese cabbage (wombok)

4 spring onions (scallions), cut into 5 cm (2 in) lengths

500 g (1 lb 2 oz) fresh wheat noodles, steamed for 15 minutes

2 tablespoons light soy sauce

Heat the oil in a wok or large heavy-based frying pan over medium heat. Add the bacon and cook for 1 minute, then add the beef, prawns, salted soy bean paste, garlic and ginger and stir-fry until the beef changes colour. Add the cabbage and spring onion and stir-fry for 1 minute, then add the noodles, soy sauce and 250 ml (8½ fl oz/1 cup) hot water. Cover and simmer for 5–8 minutes, tossing the noodles often, until all the liquid is absorbed and the noodles are soft. Serve hot.

Fried Noodles, Singapore Style

Serves: 8–10

This recipe can be prepared using fresh rice noodles (kway teow) or fresh yellow egg noodles (hokkien mee). You should prepare all the garnishes before cooking the noodles. The pork should be simply cooked – simmered in lightly salted water will do.

1 kg (2 lb 3 oz) fresh rice or hokkien mee (yellow egg) noodles

125 ml (4 fl oz/½ cup) oil

6 garlic cloves, crushed

1 tablespoon tinned salted black beans, rinsed and mashed or salted soy bean paste (taucheo)

500 g (1 lb 2 oz) pork, cooked and thinly sliced

500 g (1 lb 2 oz) raw small prawns (shrimp), peeled and deveined

1 teaspoon salt, or to taste

3 celery stalks, finely chopped

180 g (6½ oz/2 cups) fresh bean sprouts, trimmed

Garnishes

4 eggs

2 teaspoons oil

10 garlic cloves

8 spring onions (scallions), cut into 5 cm (2 in) lengths

3–4 fresh red chillies, deseeded and thinly sliced

3–4 fresh coriander (cilantro) sprigs, leaves and stalks chopped

To prepare the garnishes, beat the eggs and season with salt and freshly ground black pepper. Heat the oil in a frying pan over medium–low heat. Add the egg mixture, a little at a time, to make thin round omelettes. Do not fold, but turn them on to a plate as they are cooked. When cool, roll up and cut into thin strips.

Finely chop or pound the garlic, rinse in cold water, squeeze dry with paper towel and fry over low heat until pale golden. Lift out with a wire skimmer. Drain and cool, then crumble into small pieces. Set aside.

Prepare the noodles just before you are ready to serve. If using fresh rice noodles, cut them into 5 mm (¼ in) strips and pour boiling water over to soften and separate the layers. If using hokkien mee, rinse in hot water and drain.

Heat the oil in a wok or large heavy-based frying pan over low heat. Add the garlic and cook until it just starts to change colour. Add the black beans and stir-fry for 30 seconds.

Increase the heat to high, add the pork and cook for 1 minute, then add the prawns and continue to stir-fry for 2 minutes. Add the salt and 60 ml (2 fl oz/¼ cup) water, bring to the boil, and boil quickly for 1 minute, then add the celery and bean sprouts and toss for a further 1 minute. Add the noodles and keep tossing until all the ingredients are thoroughly mixed and the noodles heated through.

Serve the noodles on a large flat platter and sprinkle over the prepared garnishes. Serve immediately.

Note

You can serve this noodle dish with Rojak (page 199) alongside. Rojak is a piquant salad that usually accompanies fried noodles.

Mah Mee
Noodle soup

Serves: 5–6

1 tablespoon peanut oil

500 g (1 lb 2 oz) raw prawns (shrimp),
peeled and deveined (heads and shells
reserved for stock)

2 teaspoons salt

500 ml (17 fl oz/2 cups) chicken stock

1 tablespoon sesame oil

3 garlic cloves, crushed

½ teaspoon finely grated fresh ginger

125 g (4½ oz) fine egg noodles

250 g (9 oz) barbecued pork, thinly sliced

180 g (6½ oz/2 cups) fresh bean sprouts,
trimmed

1 teaspoon Chinese five-spice

130 g (4½ oz/¾ cup) crabmeat

6 spring onions (scallions), thinly sliced

1 Lebanese (short) cucumber, peeled
and diced

Heat the peanut oil in a saucepan over high heat. Add the prawn shells and heads and cook, stirring constantly, until they turn pink. Add 1 litre (34 fl oz/4 cups) water and the salt, cover, and simmer for about 30 minutes, or until reduced by a third. Strain the stock, discarding the shells and heads. Set aside. (If liked, the prawn heads and a little of the stock can be blended for a few seconds in a food processor, then passed through a fine strainer and the liquid added to the prawn stock. This results in a more flavoursome soup.) Combine the prawn and chicken stocks.

Heat the sesame oil in a clean saucepan over low heat. Add the garlic and ginger and cook until starting to brown. Add the combined stocks and the prawns, bring to the boil, then reduce the heat to low and simmer for 5 minutes. Add the noodles and continue simmering for a further 5 minutes. Add the pork, bean sprouts and Chinese five-spice, and simmer for 2 minutes to heat through and combine.

Serve the soup in bowls, garnished with the crabmeat, spring onion and cucumber.

Laksa Lemak
Mixed seafood soup

Serves: 6–8

Laksa is a one-dish meal of rice noodles and seafood in a spicy soup. The Singapore version is rich with coconut milk, while in the Penang-style version they omit the coconut milk for a piquant flavour. The former, also known as laksa lemak, is the most popular.

Prawn stock

1 tablespoon oil

shells and heads of 500 g (1 lb 2 oz) raw prawns (shrimp) (see below)

2 teaspoons salt

For the soup

375 g (13 oz) rice vermicelli (rice-stick) noodles

6 large dried red chillies, stems removed

2 tablespoons dried shrimp or 2 teaspoons dried shrimp paste

2 onions, roughly chopped

2 teaspoons grated fresh galangal or 2 teaspoons laos (dried galangal) powder

6 candlenuts or brazil nuts

2 stems lemongrass, white part only, thinly sliced, or 1 strip lemon zest

80 ml (2½ fl oz/⅓ cup) peanut oil

1 teaspoon ground turmeric

1 tablespoon ground coriander

1.5 litres (51 fl oz/6 cups) coconut milk (pages 8–9)

500 g (1 lb 2 oz) Chinese-style fish cakes, sliced (glossary)

175 g (6 oz/1 cup) crabmeat (optional)

500 g (1 lb 2 oz) raw prawns (shrimp), peeled and deveined

180 g (6½ oz/2 cups) fresh bean sprouts, trimmed, to serve

1 telegraph (long) cucumber, peeled, deseeded and thinly sliced, to serve

1 large handful Vietnamese mint leaves, to serve

Sambal ulek or Sambal bajak (page 112), to serve

fresh lime or lemon wedges (optional), to serve

To make the prawn stock, heat the oil in a saucepan over high heat. Add the prawn shells and heads and cook, stirring constantly, until they turn pink. Add 2.5 litres (85 fl oz/10 cups) water and the salt, cover, and simmer for about 30 minutes, or until reduced by a third. Strain the stock, discarding the shells and heads. Set aside.

Soak the vermicelli noodles in hot water for 10 minutes, then drain.

Soak the chillies and dried shrimp in hot water for at least 10 minutes, then drain well, reserving the soaking liquid. Place in a food processor with the onion, galangal, candlenuts and lemongrass and process to a purée, adding a little of the soaking water if needed.

Heat 60 ml (2 fl oz/¼ cup) of the peanut oil in a heavy-based saucepan over medium heat. Add the chilli mixture, stirring to prevent burning, until it darkens and becomes fragrant. Add the turmeric and coriander and stir-fry for 1 minute longer, then add the prawn stock and simmer for about 30 minutes.

Add the coconut milk to the soup, then taste and adjust the seasoning as needed. Add the fish cake and crabmeat and bring to simmering point. Add the rice vermicelli, stir to combine and heat through.

Meanwhile, heat the remaining oil in a frying pan over medium heat. Add the prawns and stir-fry for 2–3 minutes, adding a little salt to taste. Remove from the heat.

Serve the laksa in large bowls, topping each bowl with a few prawns, some of the bean sprouts, cucumber and Vietnamese mint. Serve the sambal ulek separately for intrepid chilli eaters and lime or lemon wedges for those who prefer a more piquant flavour.

Hokkien Mee Soup

Serves: 6 as a main

2 tablespoons oil

500 g (1 lb 2 oz) raw small prawns (shrimp), peeled and deveined

500 g (1 lb 2 oz) hokkien mee (yellow egg) noodles

125 g (4½ oz) rice vermicelli (rice-stick) noodles

390 g (14 oz/4⅓ cups) fresh bean sprouts, trimmed

12 spinach leaves

2 litres (68 fl oz/8 cups) pork or chicken stock

2 dried red chillies, deseeded

sugar, to taste

soy sauce, to taste

salt, to taste

125 g (4½ oz) pork fat, diced and lightly fried, to serve

4 tablespoons Fried onion flakes (page 105), to serve

4 dried red chillies (optional), deseeded and lightly fried, to serve

Heat 1 tablespoon of the oil in a frying pan over medium–high heat. Add the prawns and cook until they start to turn pink, then remove to a plate. Parboil the hokkien mee noodles in a saucepan of boiling water, then drain and run cold water over them to stop the cooking process. Remove to a plate. Soak the rice vermicelli in hot water for 10 minutes, then drain well and set aside. Scald the bean sprouts by pouring boiling water over them in a colander, then run cold water over to cool and set aside. Blanch the spinach briefly in a little boiling water until half cooked, then drain and cut into short strips. Set aside.

Put the stock into a saucepan and bring to the boil.

Heat the remaining oil in a separate large saucepan and cook the chillies, until they darken, then add the hot stock, sugar, soy sauce and salt, to taste, and simmer for 5 minutes.

To serve the soup, divide the noodles, rice vermicelli, bean sprouts, prawns and spinach leaves between bowls. Pour the boiling soup over the top, then serve with the pork, onion flakes, crumbled fried chillies and extra soy sauce on the table so each person can add to their soup according to their own taste.

Spring Rolls

Makes: 20

This popular snack is within the scope of any home cook now that spring roll wrappers are available frozen from Asian grocery stores. Thaw them before attempting to separate these delicate pastry squares.

6 dried shiitake mushrooms

1 tablespoon peanut oil

1 tablespoon sesame oil

1 garlic clove, crushed

½ teaspoon finely grated fresh ginger

250 g (9 oz) pork, finely chopped

250 g (9 oz) raw prawns (shrimp), peeled, deveined and chopped

150 g (5½ oz/2 cups) shredded Chinese cabbage (wombok)

75 g (2¾ oz/¾ cup) shredded daikon (white radish)

12 tinned water chestnuts, drained and chopped

250 g (9 oz/1 cup) chopped bamboo shoots

90 g (3 oz/1 cup) fresh bean sprouts, trimmed

6 spring onions (scallions), thinly sliced

1 tablespoon light soy sauce

1 tablespoon oyster sauce

1 teaspoon salt

3 teaspoons cornflour (cornstarch)

20 spring roll wrappers

oil for deep-frying

Soak the mushrooms in hot water for 20–30 minutes. Drain well, remove the stalks and finely chop the caps. Heat the peanut and sesame oils in a wok and cook the garlic and ginger for a few seconds. Increase the heat, add the pork, and stir-fry until it changes colour. Add the prawns and stir-fry until they are cooked. Add the vegetables, soy sauce, oyster sauce and salt, and stir to combine. Push the mixture to one side of the wok.

Combine the cornflour and water and stir to make a smooth paste. Add to the wok and stir until the sauce thickens. Remove from the heat and stir to combine. Allow to cool completely.

Put 2 tablespoons of the mixture at one end of the spring roll wrapper and roll up, folding in the sides so that the filling is completely enclosed. Dampen the edges with water or a mixture of cornflour and water and press to seal.

Heat the oil in a large heavy-based frying pan over medium heat. When the oil is hot, deep-fry the spring rolls, in batches, until golden brown. Drain on paper towel and serve straight away with Chilli sauce (page 198), if desired.

Murtaba
Rotis with savoury filling

Makes: 10–12

Rotis

150 g (5½ oz/1 cup) roti flour or plain (all-purpose) flour

1 teaspoon salt

1 tablespoon ghee or oil

125 ml (4 fl oz/½ cup) oil

Filling

40 g (1½ oz) ghee

1 large onion, thinly sliced

2 garlic cloves, crushed

½ teaspoon finely grated fresh ginger

1 teaspoon ground turmeric

½ teaspoon chilli powder

500 g (1 lb 2 oz) minced (ground) lamb or goat

1 teaspoon garam masala

1½ teaspoons salt

2 eggs, lightly beaten (optional)

salt and freshly ground black pepper

1 onion, thinly sliced

Put the flour and salt in a bowl and rub in 1 tablespoon of ghee. Add 250 ml (8½ fl oz/1 cup) lukewarm water all at once and mix to a fairly soft dough. Turn out onto a clean work surface and knead the dough for at least 10 minutes. Divide into 10 even-sized balls and place them in a bowl with the oil so they are covered and leave to rest for 1 hour.

Heat 40 g (1½ oz) of ghee in a large heavy-based frying pan over low heat. Add the onion and cook until it softens. Add the garlic and ginger and cook until the onion is golden brown. Add the turmeric and chilli powder and stir for a few seconds, then add the mince and cook, turning the meat constantly to break up any large lumps, until it starts to brown. Cover and cook for 15 minutes. Add the garam masala and salt and continue cooking until the meat and peas are tender and the mixture is quite dry.

Season the eggs well with salt and pepper. You can have a choice of fillings, or use some beaten egg and some meat together.

Heat a little of the oil on a griddle plate or in a large heavy-based frying pan over medium heat.

On a clean work surface, spread a little oil from the bowl and roll out the dough balls with a rolling pin. Gently press with fingers, spreading the dough until it is quite thin. Drape the roti over a rolling pin and carry it to the griddle, placing it on the hot surface much as you would put the top on a pie. It will cook very quickly, so spoon on some beaten egg and spread it over the middle portion of the roti with the underside of the spoon. Sprinkle some meat over and finally add a few slices of onion. Fold over the sides of the roti, envelope-fashion, to completely enclose the filling, then turn with a spatula and cook the other side, spreading a little more ghee or oil on the griddle before you put it down. When crisp and golden on both sides it is ready. Remove from the heat and keep warm while you cook the remainder. Serve hot.

Sometimes the murtaba is cooked without any filling and served with a curry, in which case it is broken, dipped and eaten in the same way as chapati or paratha.

Poh Pia

Fresh spring rolls

Makes: about 25

....

Egg roll wrappers

5 eggs

1 teaspoon salt

2 tablespoons oil, plus extra for cooking

150 g (5½ oz/1 cup) plain (all-purpose) flour

Filling

80 ml (2½ fl oz/⅓ cup) oil

190 g (6½ oz) firm tofu, cut in strips

500 g (1 lb 2 oz) pork belly, boiled and diced

6 garlic cloves, finely chopped

3 tablespoons salted soy beans, drained and mashed, or salted soy bean paste (taucheo)

250 g (9 oz) raw prawns (shrimp), peeled, deveined and chopped

500 g (1 lb 2 oz/2 cups) bamboo shoots, cut into matchsticks

750 g (1 lb 11 oz) yam bean (jicama), peeled and cut into matchsticks

½ teaspoon salt, or to taste

Garnishes

3 eggs, lightly beaten

10–15 garlic cloves

1 large lettuce, leaves separated

175 g (6 oz/1 cup) crabmeat, flaked

1 Lebanese (short) cucumber, peeled, deseeded and thinly sliced into strips

180 g (6½ oz/2 cups) fresh bean sprouts, trimmed

6 Chinese sausages (lap cheong), steamed and sliced

1 small handful fresh coriander (cilantro) leaves

chilli sauce

kecap manis

To prepare the garnishes, beat the eggs and season with salt and freshly ground black pepper. Heat the oil in a frying pan over medium heat. Add the egg mixture, a little at a time, to make thin round omelettes. Do not fold, but turn them onto a plate as they are cooked. When cool, roll up and cut into thin strips.

Finely chop or pound the garlic, rinse in cold water, then squeeze dry with paper towel. Heat a little oil in a frying pan and cook over low heat until golden. Lift out with a wire skimmer. Drain and cool, then crumble into small pieces. Set aside.

To make the egg roll wrappers, whisk together the eggs and 375 ml (12½ fl oz/1½ cups) cold water in a bowl until well combined but not too frothy. Add the salt, oil and flour and beat until smooth. Allow to rest for 30 minutes.

Lightly oil a heavy-based frying pan or pancake pan. Pour in a small ladle of the wrapper mixture and swirl to thinly coat the base of the pan. Cook over low heat until the underside is cooked and pale golden. Turn and cook the other side for a few seconds only – these wrappers should not be allowed to brown. Remove to a plate and repeat until all the batter is used – you should make about 25 wrappers in total.

To make the filling, heat the oil in a wok or large heavy-based frying pan over medium heat. Add the tofu strips and stir-fry until they are golden brown all over. Drain on paper towel and cut into small dice. Pour off all but 1 tablespoon of the oil from the wok, add the pork and stir-fry until the fat begins to run. Add the garlic and salted soy beans and stir-fry until the garlic is golden. Add the prawns and toss until they turn pink. Add the bamboo shoots and yam bean and stir-fry until cooked but still crisp, then return the tofu to the pan; season with salt, to taste, and simmer until the filling is almost dry. Remove from the heat and drain off any remaining oil from the filling.

Assembling the poh pia is half the fun and adds greatly to the enjoyment of eating this snack. Each person puts an egg roll wrapper on his or her plate. On this goes a piece of lettuce leaf, which is then spread with chilli sauce or sprinkled with the kecap manis. A spoonful of the cooked filling is then put on the leaf and garnishes, as desired, are added. Roll up the egg wrapper, turning in the sides so that the filling is completely enclosed. Poh pia should be eaten immediately.

Fish and Seafood

Stir-Fried Prawns with Bean Sprouts and Snow Peas

Serves: 4–6

2 tablespoons dried wood ear fungus

2 tablespoons oil

1 garlic clove, crushed

½ teaspoon finely grated fresh ginger

2 celery stalks, thinly sliced

180 g (6½ oz/2 cups) fresh bean sprouts, trimmed

250 g (9 oz) raw small prawns (shrimp), peeled and deveined

12–18 snow peas (mangetout), trimmed and thinly sliced

2 teaspoons cornflour (cornstarch)

1 teaspoon sugar

1 tablespoon light soy sauce

1 tablespoon Chinese rice wine or dry sherry

Soak the wood ear fungus in hot water for 10 minutes. It will swell and soften. Trim off any gritty pieces.

Heat 1 tablespoon of the oil in a wok or large heavy-based frying pan over high heat. Add the garlic and ginger and stir-fry for 10 seconds, then add the celery and stir-fry for 2 minutes. Add the bean sprouts and stir-fry for 1 minute, or until the vegetables are tender but still crisp. Remove to a plate.

Add the remaining oil to the wok and stir-fry the prawns until they turn pink. Add the snow peas and stir-fry for 30–40 seconds. Return the other vegetables to the wok with the wood ear fungus and toss until heated through, then move them to the side of the wok. Add the cornflour to the liquid in the base of the pan and stir through the sugar, soy sauce and wine to combine then toss the vegetables back through the sauce. Serve immediately.

Sweet and Sour Fried Prawns

Serves: 4

Soaking the prawns (shrimp) in cold salted water is a Chinese technique that gives the prawns a wonderfully springy texture.

500 g (1 lb 2 oz) raw prawns (shrimp), peeled and deveined, tails left intact

1 teaspoon salt

½ teaspoon finely grated fresh ginger

2 egg whites

2½ tablespoons cornflour (cornstarch)

peanut oil for deep-frying

1 Lebanese (short) cucumber, thinly sliced

Sauce

60 ml (2 fl oz/¼ cup) white vinegar

190 ml (6½ fl oz/¾ cup) pineapple or orange juice

1 tablespoon sugar

½ teaspoon salt

a pinch of red colouring powder (optional)

1 tablespoon arrowroot

Wash the prawns, then soak them in a bowl with 750 ml (25½ fl oz/3 cups) cold water and ½ teaspoon of the salt for 30 minutes. Drain well in a colander and then pat dry with paper towel. Put the prawns into a dry bowl and sprinkle with the remaining salt. Add the ginger and toss to coat. Add the egg whites and cornflour and mix again until the prawns are well coated. Cover and refrigerate for at least 4 hours or overnight.

To make the sauce, combine the vinegar, pineapple juice, sugar and salt in a bowl and add just enough colouring to give a bright pink colour, if desired. Bring to the boil, then remove from the heat. In a small bowl, combine the arrowroot with 1 tablespoon cold water and stir to make a smooth paste. Add to the pan, return to the heat and stir until the sauce boils and thickens.

Heat the peanut oil in a large heavy-based saucepan over medium heat. When the oil is hot, deep-fry the prawns, in batches, for 1 minute or until they turn pink. Do not overcook or they will become tough. Lift out with a slotted spoon and drain on paper towel. To serve, put the prawns on a serving plate and pour over the hot sauce. Garnish with the cucumber.

Fish and Seafood

Fried Fish with Crab Sauce

Serves: 5–6

1 kg (2 lb 3 oz) skinless, boneless,
  firm white fish fillets

½ teaspoon finely grated fresh ginger

1 teaspoon salt

2 teaspoons cornflour (cornstarch)

peanut oil for deep-frying

Sauce

2 tablespoons peanut oil

6 spring onions (scallions), thinly sliced

½ teaspoon finely grated fresh ginger

250 ml (8½ fl oz/1 cup) chicken or
  fish stock

175 g (6 oz/1 cup) crabmeat

1 pinch of freshly ground black pepper

2½ teaspoons cornflour (cornstarch)

Wipe the fish with damp paper towel. Rub the grated ginger over the fish, then cut each fillet into bite-sized pieces. Combine the salt and cornflour in a bowl and toss to coat the fish.

Heat the peanut oil in a large heavy-based frying pan over medium heat. When the oil is hot, deep-fry the fish, a few pieces at a time, for 1 minute, or until opaque. Drain on paper towel and keep warm while preparing the sauce.

To make the sauce, heat the peanut oil in a saucepan over medium–low heat. Add the spring onion and ginger and stir-fry for a few seconds, then add the stock, reduce the heat to low, cover, and simmer for 3–4 minutes. Add the crabmeat and heat through for no longer than a minute; season with the pepper, to taste. Mix together the cornflour and 1 tablespoon cold water in a bowl until smooth, then add to the pan and stir to combine. Bring back to the boil and season, to taste. Arrange the fish on a serving plate with the hot sauce spooned over the top and serve immediately.

Deep-Fried Fish with Vegetables

Serves: 4–6

750 g (1 lb 11 oz) skinless, boneless, firm white fish fillets

1 teaspoon salt

½ teaspoon Chinese five-spice

1 tablespoon cornflour (cornstarch), plus 1 teaspoon extra

1 tablespoon egg white

125 ml (4 fl oz/½ cup) oil

1 garlic clove, crushed

½ teaspoon finely grated fresh ginger

150 g (5½ oz/2 cups) sliced Chinese cabbage (wombok)

6 spring onions (scallions), cut into 5 cm (2 in) lengths

1 tablespoon light soy sauce

1 tablespoon oyster sauce

Wipe the fish with damp paper towel. Cut the fish into serving pieces (see page 13). Combine the salt, five-spice and cornflour in one bowl. Put the egg white in another bowl.

Heat the oil in a large heavy-based frying pan over medium heat. Dip the fish pieces first in the egg white and then toss in the cornflour mixture, shaking off any excess. When the oil is hot, deep-fry the fish, in batches, for 1–2 minutes, until just cooked through and crisp. Drain on paper towel and keep warm while preparing the sauce.

Pour off all but 1 tablespoon of the oil from the pan, add the garlic, ginger and cabbage and stir-fry for 1 minute. Add the spring onion and stir-fry for 1 minute, then add the soy sauce, oyster sauce and 125 ml (4 fl oz/½ cup) water and bring to the boil. In a small bowl, combine the extra cornflour and 1 tablespoon water to make a smooth paste. Add to the pan and stir until the sauce boils and thickens.

Arrange the fish on serving plates with the hot sauce spooned over the top and serve immediately with rice or noodles.

Fish and Seafood ❖

Fried Chilli Crabs

Serves: 4

2 raw blue swimmer or mud crabs

125 ml (4 fl oz/½ cup) peanut oil

2 teaspoons finely grated fresh ginger

3 garlic cloves, finely chopped

3 fresh red chillies, deseeded and chopped

60 ml (2 fl oz/¼ cup) tomato sauce
 (ketchup)

60 ml (2 fl oz/¼ cup) chilli sauce

1 tablespoon sugar

1 tablespoon light soy sauce

1 teaspoon salt

If using live crabs, place them in the freezer for at least one hour before cooking in order to put them to sleep.

Remove the large shells from the crabs and discard the fibrous tissue under the shell. Divide each crab into 4 portions, breaking each body in half and separating the claws from the body, leaving the legs attached.

Heat the peanut oil in a wok or large heavy-based frying pan over medium–high heat. Add the crab pieces and cook, turning regularly, until they change colour on all sides. Remove to a plate.

Reduce the heat to low and cook the ginger, garlic and chilli, stirring constantly, until they are cooked but not brown. Add the tomato and chilli sauces, sugar, soy sauce and salt, bring to the boil. Reduce the heat to low, return the crab pieces to the wok and allow to simmer in the sauce for 3 minutes, adding a little water if the sauce reduces too much. Serve with white rice.

Prawns in Chilli Bean Sauce

Serves: 2–3

....

1 garlic clove, crushed with ½ teaspoon salt

½ teaspoon finely grated fresh ginger

2 teaspoons Chinese rice wine or dry sherry

12 raw large prawns (shrimp), peeled
    and deveined

1 tablespoon tinned salted black beans,
    rinsed and crushed

1–2 teaspoons chilli sauce

2 teaspoons hoisin sauce

2 tablespoons peanut oil

1 red capsicum (bell pepper), deseeded
    and chopped

1 green capsicum (bell pepper), deseeded
    and chopped

1 spring onion (scallion), thinly sliced,
    to garnish

Mix together the garlic, ginger and wine in a bowl. Add the prawns and set aside to marinate while preparing the other ingredients.

Combine the black beans and chilli and hoisin sauces in a bowl.

Heat the peanut oil in a wok or large heavy-based frying pan over high heat. Add the capsicum and stir-fry for 2 minutes, then move them to the side of the wok. Add the prawns and stir-fry for 2–3 minutes, or until they turn pink. Move the prawns to one side of the wok, then add the black bean mixture and stir-fry for 30 seconds. Toss all the ingredients together to coat. Serve hot, garnished with the spring onion.

Deep Fried Prawns with Chilli

Serves: 4

oil for deep-frying

500 g (1 lb 2 oz) raw prawns (shrimp),
  peeled and deveined

3 fresh red chillies, deseeded and chopped

1 garlic clove

2 teaspoons finely grated fresh ginger

1 tablespoon sugar

1 tablespoon light soy sauce

1 tablespoon Chinese rice wine or
  dry sherry

Heat the oil in a wok or large heavy-based saucepan over medium heat. When the oil is hot, deep-fry the prawns, in batches, for 2–3 minutes, or just until they turn pink. Remove to a plate and drain on paper towel.

Pour off all but 1 tablespoon of oil from the wok. Combine the chilli, garlic and ginger in a bowl with 1 teaspoon of the sugar. Add to the wok and stir-fry over low heat, then add the remaining sugar, soy sauce and wine and stir well to combine. Return the prawns to the wok and stir to combine and heat through. Serve immediately with rice or noodles.

Meat

❖

Crisp Skin Chicken

Serves: 4

This is a recipe that I have pursued for years – there are many versions and I wouldn't be surprised if I've tried them all in my search for perfection! When you have a few hours to spare between planning your meal and eating it, you may care to try this method … I'm sure the results will be pleasing.

1 kg (2 lb 3 oz) whole chicken

1 teaspoon salt, plus extra to serve

2¼ teaspoons Chinese five-spice, plus extra to serve

1 teaspoon cayenne pepper

2 teaspoons ground cinnamon

1 tablespoon honey

1 lemon, sliced

2 litres (68 fl oz/8 cups) oil

lemon wedges, to serve

fresh coriander (cilantro) leaves, to serve

Wash the chicken and remove the neck and giblets. Pat dry with paper towel inside and out. Rub inside the chicken with the combined salt and ¼ teaspoon of the five-spice.

Put 1.5 litres (51 fl oz/6 cups) water in a large saucepan with the cayenne pepper, cinnamon and remaining five-spice and bring to the boil. Remove from the heat and pour over the chicken in a bowl. Set aside.

Put 1 litre (34 fl oz/4 cups) water in a clean saucepan with the honey and lemon slices and bring to the boil. Remove from the heat.

Drain the chicken from the first mixture and put it in a colander. Pour the honey mixture over the top of the chicken, making sure it comes into contact with all parts of the skin. Put the chicken on a wire rack in front of an electric fan to dry for 1 hour or until all the skin is dry to the touch.

Just before serving, heat the oil in a wok over medium heat. Tie the legs of the chicken together, leaving some string to hold it with, and carefully lower the bird into the hot oil. With a ladle, spoon the oil over the chicken as it cooks, and turn it so that it is cooked and brown on all sides, about 12–15 minutes. Test by piercing with a fine skewer where the thigh joins the body – if the juice runs clear the chicken is done. Lift onto a board using a slotted spoon and cut the chicken in half lengthways with a heavy meat cleaver. Place each half, cut side down, on the board and chop into 2.5 cm (1 in) strips, then reassemble the bird on a serving dish.

Serve with lemon wedges and some combined salt and five-spice. Garnish with the coriander and serve immediately. The pieces of chicken are sprinkled with the spice mix and lemon juice by the diners before eating, according to taste.

Country Captain

Serves: 4–6

1.5 kg (3 lb 5 oz) whole chicken or
  chicken pieces

2 garlic cloves, crushed with 2 teaspoons salt

1 teaspoon ground turmeric

½ teaspoon freshly ground black pepper

80 ml (2½ fl oz/⅓ cup) oil

4 large onions, thinly sliced

2 fresh red chillies, deseeded and sliced

Joint the chicken (see page 13) and cut into serving pieces.

Combine the garlic, turmeric and pepper and rub over the chicken pieces to coat.

Heat the oil in a large heavy-based saucepan over low heat. Add half of the onion and cook until brown. Remove to a plate.

Add the remaining onion to the pan with the chilli and stir-fry until just starting to colour, then add the chicken to the pan and cook, turning regularly, until golden all over. Add 125 ml (4 fl oz/½ cup) water, cover, and simmer gently until the chicken is tender. Uncover, and continue simmering until all the liquid has evaporated. Serve hot, garnished with the reserved fried onion and accompanied by fried potatoes or boiled rice.

Satay-Flavoured Roast Chicken

Serves: 4–5

1 onion, roughly chopped

1 garlic clove

2 fresh red chillies, deseeded and chopped

500 ml (17 fl oz/2 cups) coconut milk
(pages 8–9)

2 teaspoons ground coriander

1½ teaspoons ground cumin

½ teaspoon ground fennel

½ teaspoon ground turmeric

½ teaspoon laos (dried galangal) powder
(optional)

½ teaspoon finely grated lemon zest

2 candlenuts or brazil nuts, finely grated

2 tablespoons oil or ghee

1½ teaspoons salt

1 tablespoon lemon juice

1.5 kg (3 lb 5 oz) whole chicken

Put the onion, garlic and chilli into a food processor and process to a smooth paste, adding 2 tablespoons of the coconut milk if necessary. Mix in the ground spices, lemon zest and candlenuts.

Preheat the oven to 180°C (350°F).

Heat the oil in a large heavy-based saucepan over low heat. Add the chilli mixture and stir-fry until the colour darkens and the oil starts to separate. Remove from the heat and stir in the salt and lemon juice. Allow to cool slightly.

Rub the spice mixture inside and outside the chicken, truss the chicken, and place in a deep roasting tin, breast side up. Pour the coconut milk around the chicken and roast in the oven for 15 minutes then, basting with the liquid in the tin, turn the chicken so that it is breast side down and cook for a further 1¼ hours, or until tender. You will need to continue basting the chicken every 20 minutes or so during cooking; if the coconut milk shows signs of drying up, add up to 250 ml (8½ fl oz/1 cup) more. Towards the end of cooking, turn the chicken, breast side up, and continue cooking for a further 15 minutes, or until it is a nice golden brown and cooked through. Carve the chicken and serve with the coconut milk spooned over the top. Serve with rice and other accompaniments.

Pork with Sichuan Vegetables

Serves: 3–4

125 g (4½ oz) rice vermicelli (rice-stick) noodles

2 tablespoons oil

250 g (9 oz) pork loin, diced

5 garlic cloves, finely chopped

2 teaspoons finely grated fresh ginger

3 tablespoons chopped tinned sichuan vegetables (see mustard cabbage entry in glossary)

5 leaves Chinese cabbage (wombok), sliced

1 teaspoon light soy sauce

190 ml (6½ fl oz/¾ cup) pork stock or water

Soak the rice vermicelli noodles according to the packet instructions, then drain well.

Heat the oil in a wok or large heavy-based frying pan over medium–high heat. Add the pork and stir-fry until brown and crisp. Drain on paper towel.

Pour off all but 1 tablespoon of the oil from the pan and cook the garlic, ginger and sichuan vegetables over medium heat until the garlic and ginger are soft and golden. Add the cabbage and stir-fry for 2 minutes, then add the soy sauce and stock and bring to the boil. Add the rice vermicelli and cook until all the liquid is absorbed. Stir through the pork until heated through. Serve hot.

Eastern-Style Croquettes

Makes: about 18

2 tablespoons oil, plus extra for deep-frying

1 onion, finely chopped

2 garlic cloves, finely chopped

½ teaspoon finely grated fresh ginger

2 fresh green chillies, deseeded and chopped

2 teaspoons ground coriander

1 teaspoon ground cumin

500 g (1 lb 2 oz) minced (ground) beef

1½ teaspoons salt, plus extra to taste

½ teaspoon freshly ground black pepper, plus extra to taste

2 tablespoons finely chopped fresh coriander (cilantro) leaves

6 spring onions (scallions), finely chopped

1 kg (2 lb 3 oz) potatoes, boiled and mashed

1 egg, beaten

dry breadcrumbs for coating

Heat the oil in a wok or large heavy-based frying pan over low heat. Add the onion, garlic, ginger and chilli and stir-fry until soft. Add the ground coriander, cumin and beef and cook, breaking up any large lumps of meat, until the meat changes colour. Add the salt and pepper, cover, and cook until meat is tender. (There should be no liquid left when the meat is cooked.) Stir in the coriander leaves and allow to cool. When cold, stir in the spring onion.

Season the mashed potato with salt and pepper, to taste. Take 2 tablespoons of mashed potato in one hand, flatten slightly, then put 1 tablespoon of meat mixture in the centre. Mould the potato around the meat to form an oval shape, known as a croquette, enclosing the meat. Set aside on a large tray and repeat with the remaining meat and potato.

Heat the extra oil in a large heavy-based frying pan over medium heat. Dip each croquette first in the egg, then in the breadcrumbs, shaking off any excess. When the oil is hot, deep-fry the croquettes, in batches, until golden brown. Drain on paper towel and serve hot with chilli sauce.

Fried Pork with Rice Vermicelli

Serves: 4

....

250 g (9 oz) fine rice vermicelli (rice-stick) noodles

80 ml (2½ fl oz/⅓ cup) peanut oil

155 g (5½ oz/1 cup) cubed raw potato

2 onions, thinly sliced

3 garlic cloves, finely chopped

250 g (9 oz) pork belly, skin removed and meat diced

2 tablespoons light soy sauce

freshly ground black pepper, to taste

¼ teaspoon salt

3 teaspoons sugar

Soak the rice vermicelli noodles according to the packet instructions, then drain well.

Heat the peanut oil in a wok or large heavy-based frying pan over high heat. Add the potato and stir-fry for 2 minutes. Reduce the heat to medium and continue stir-frying until the potato is golden all over. Remove to a plate.

Add the onion and garlic to the wok and stir-fry for 2 minutes, then add the pork and stir-fry for a further 5 minutes, or until the pork is cooked and golden brown. Combine the soy sauce and 125 ml (4 fl oz/½ cup) water and add half of this mixture to the wok with the vermicelli. Continue cooking until the water is absorbed, then add the remaining sauce and water with the pepper, salt and sugar, and stir until the liquid is almost all absorbed, taking care not to let the vermicelli stick to the base of the wok. Stir in the potatoes and heat through. Serve hot.

Pork or Beef Satay

Serves: 4

1 strip lemon zest

2 onions, roughly chopped

1 tablespoon light soy sauce

1–2 tablespoons oil

2 teaspoons ground coriander

1 teaspoon ground cumin

1 teaspoon ground turmeric

¼ teaspoon ground cinnamon

1 teaspoon salt

1 teaspoon sugar

2 tablespoons roasted peanuts

500 g (1 lb 2 oz) pork fillet or rump steak, cut into small cubes

Soak 8 bamboo skewers in cold water to prevent them from burning during cooking.

Put the lemon zest, onion, soy sauce and 1 tablespoon of the oil into a food processor and process until smooth, then add the remaining ingredients, except the meat, and blend for a few seconds longer, adding the remaining oil if necessary. Pour over the meat in a bowl, tossing to coat, and leave to marinate for at least 1 hour.

Thread about 6 cubes of meat onto each skewer and grill over glowing coals or under a preheated grill (broiler) until brown all over and the meat is cooked. Serve with peanut sauce, white rice and a salad.

Spiced Spareribs

Serves: 6

This recipe is a favourite of mine, as not only is it easy to prepare, but the flavour so special and it can be prepared a day ahead. When required, grill (broil) the spareribs a few minutes on each side, just to heat through. The best way to enjoy spareribs is to pick them up with your fingers.

4 garlic cloves, crushed with 1½ teaspoons salt

½ teaspoon freshly ground black pepper

½ teaspoon Chinese five-spice

1 tablespoon honey

1 tablespoon sesame oil

60 ml (2 fl oz/¼ cup) light soy sauce

1.5 kg (3 lb 5 oz) pork spareribs, separated (ask your butcher to do this)

plum sauce, to serve

Preheat the oven to 180°C (350°F). Combine the garlic, pepper, five-spice, honey, sesame oil and soy sauce in a bowl. Add the spareribs and rub well to coat. Put the spareribs in a roasting tin and cook in the oven for 30 minutes, then turn the spareribs over, add 125 ml (4 fl oz/½ cup) hot water to the tin and continue roasting for a further 30 minutes, basting with the liquid every 10 minutes or so.

Alternatively, heat 1–2 tablespoons peanut oil in a large heavy-based frying pan and brown the spareribs on all sides. Add the hot water, cover, and simmer for 30–35 minutes, or until tender and cooked through. Serve hot with rice and plum sauce.

Barbecue-Style Pork with Black Beans

Serves: 6

3 garlic cloves, crushed with ½ teaspoon salt

1 teaspoon finely grated fresh ginger

1 tablespoon honey

1 tablespoon Chinese rice wine or
dry sherry

½ teaspoon Chinese five-spice

1 tablespoon tinned salted black beans,
rinsed and chopped

1 tablespoon dark soy sauce

1 tablespoon Chinese barbecue (char siu)
sauce

750 g (1 lb 11 oz) boneless pork loin,
trimmed and cut into thin strips

1 tablespoon peanut oil

Combine all the ingredients, except for the pork and oil in a bowl. Add the pork, toss to coat and leave to marinate for at least 15 minutes. Drain, reserving the marinade.

Heat the oil in a wok or large heavy-based frying pan over medium heat. Add the pork and stir-fry until browned, then add the reserved marinade and 125 ml (4 fl oz/½ cup) hot water. Reduce the heat to low, cover, and simmer for 30–40 minutes, or until the pork is tender – you may need to add more hot water if the liquid looks like it is drying up. Be careful that the sweet marinade does not burn. The heat should be very low throughout the cooking. Serve hot with plain white rice.

Sambal Babi

Pork and hot spices in coconut milk

Serves: 6–8

Sambals are traditionally hot and spicy, but they needn't be. Even without chilli this curry is very rich and intensely flavoured. The coconut milk smooths out the strong flavours. Once you know your chilli tolerance you can adjust the chilli content to suit.

750 g (1 lb 11 oz) pork belly

375 ml (12½ fl oz/1½ cups) thick coconut milk (pages 8–9)

1 stem lemongrass, bruised, or 1 strip lemon zest

1½ teaspoons finely chopped fresh galangal or laos (dried galangal) powder

2 teaspoons finely grated fresh ginger

2 small onions, finely chopped

4 garlic cloves, crushed

1–2 teaspoons chilli powder

1 teaspoon dried shrimp paste

1 teaspoon ground coriander

1 teaspoon ground cumin

1–2 teaspoons sugar, or to taste

1 teaspoon salt

Cut the pork, skin and all, into small cubes. Put the pork, and all the other ingredients into a large saucepan and bring to the boil, stirring constantly – this prevents the coconut milk curdling. Reduce the heat to low and simmer for about 1 hour, or until the pork is tender and the liquid is almost absorbed, stirring frequently.

Serve with white rice and other accompaniments, such as cooling salads. Reduce the quantity of chilli if a less volcanic result is preferred.

Accompaniments

Satay Sauce

Makes: 2 cups

80 ml (2½ fl oz/⅓ cup) oil

1 stem lemongrass, white part only, sliced and crushed, or 2 teaspoons finely grated lemon zest

1 onion, finely chopped

3 garlic cloves, finely chopped

2 teaspoons dried shrimp paste

200 g (7 oz/1¼ cups) roasted peanuts

2 tablespoons tamarind pulp

1 teaspoon chilli powder

1½ teaspoons laos (dried galangal) powder

2 tablespoons sugar

1 teaspoon salt

Put 2 tablespoons of the oil in a food processor with the lemongrass, onion, garlic and dried shrimp paste and process to a paste. Scrape out the food processor, reserving the onion mixture and then process the peanuts until finely crushed. Set aside.

Soak the tamarind pulp in 250 ml (8½ fl oz/1 cup) hot water for 10 minutes. Squeeze to dissolve the pulp in the water, then strain, discarding the seeds and fibre.

Heat the remaining oil in a wok or large heavy-based frying pan over medium heat. Add the onion mixture and stir until heated through, then add the chilli powder, laos powder, tamarind liquid, sugar, salt and peanuts. Simmer for about 8 minutes, stirring until thickened, then use as directed.

Chilli Sauce

Makes: 3 cups

This chilli sauce may be sweet but it still packs a punch, especially if you leave the seeds in the chillies.

250 g (9 oz) fresh red chillies, deseeded
  and chopped

750 ml (25½ fl oz/3 cups) white vinegar

660 g (1 lb 7 oz/3 cups) sugar

280 g (10 oz/2¼ cups) sultanas
  (golden raisins)

8 garlic cloves

3 teaspoons salt, or to taste

1 tablespoon finely grated fresh ginger

Using a food processor, process the chilli with enough of the vinegar to facilitate processing. Transfer to a large stainless-steel saucepan, add the remaining ingredients and bring to the boil. Reduce the heat to low and simmer until the sultanas and chilli are very soft. Cool, then transfer to a food processor and process to a smooth purée. Pour into sterilised airtight jars and store for up to 6 months.

Note

You can use 50 g (1¾ oz/½ cup) chilli powder instead of fresh chillies if fresh are unavailable.

Rojak

Serves: 8–10

1 telegraph (long) cucumber, peeled, deseeded and thinly sliced

1 small pineapple, skin and core removed, flesh diced

3 fresh red or green chillies, deseeded and thinly sliced

salt

Dressing

1 teaspoon dried shrimp paste, or to taste

3 tablespoons Chinese rice vinegar or other mild vinegar

2 tablespoons sugar

2 teaspoons Sambal ulek (page 104) or crushed fresh chillies

lemon juice, to taste

Combine the cucumber, pineapple and chilli in a bowl and sprinkle lightly with salt.

To make the dressing, wrap the dried shrimp paste in a piece of foil and roast under a preheated grill (broiler) for 5 minutes, turning halfway through. Unwrap and add to a bowl with the vinegar, stirring to dissolve. Add the sugar and sambal ulek, and season with salt and lemon juice to taste. Pour the dressing over the pineapple mixture and toss to coat or serve the dressing separately.

Sweets
and
Desserts

❀

Almond Biscuits

Makes: about 16

Lard, along with dripping, was once widely used in Western cuisines until we became conscious of cholesterol levels, and animal fats were replaced by unsaturated vegetable oils. However, nothing else will give these biscuits (cookies) their unique texture and flavour. If you can't eat lard, try replacing it with extra-virgin coconut oil. It's not the same, but delicious in its own way.

125 g (4½ oz) lard, softened, or 125 ml (4 fl oz/½ cup) coconut oil

115 g (4 oz/½ cup) caster (superfine) sugar

1 teaspoon natural almond extract

3–4 drops yellow food colouring (optional)

225 g (8 oz/1½ cups) plain (all-purpose) flour

8 blanched almonds

1 egg yolk

Preheat the oven to 160°C (320°F). Lightly grease two baking trays.

Beat together the lard and sugar until light and creamy. Add the almond extract and, if liked, a little colouring. Gradually add the flour, stirring well to combine. After adding the last of the flour it will be necessary to work the mixture with your hands, but it will still be a crumbly consistency.

Take 1 tablespoon of the mixture at a time and shape into flat circles with a 5 cm (2 in) diameter – the edges of each circle will have little cracks in them. Place on the prepared trays.

Put the almonds in a small saucepan with enough water to cover and bring to the boil. Remove from the heat, drain well, then split each almond in half.

Press an almond into the centre of each biscuit. Beat together the egg yolk and 1 tablespoon water and brush over the top of each biscuit (cookie). Bake in the oven for 30 minutes, or until pale golden. Cool slightly on the trays, then transfer to a wire rack to cool completely. Store in an airtight container for up to 10 days.

Toffee Apples

Makes: 24 pieces

These toffee apples are thick slices of apple fried in batter, then dropped into a sugar glaze with black sesame seeds, hardened quickly in a bowl of iced water and eaten with chopsticks.

1 egg, lightly beaten

150 g (5½ oz/1 cup) plain (all-purpose) flour

peanut oil for deep-frying

3 cooking apples, such as granny smith or pink lady, peeled, cored and cut into 8 wedges each

ice cubes and water for dipping

Glaze

225 g (8 oz/1½ cups) sugar

2 teaspoons black sesame seeds

Beat together the egg and 170 ml (5½ fl oz/⅔ cup) water in a bowl until combined, then tip in all the flour at once and beat vigorously until the batter is smooth – do not overbeat. Set aside.

To make the glaze, put the sugar and 125 ml (4 fl oz/½ cup) cold water into a small saucepan over medium–high heat. Do not stir or the sugar will crystallise and the glaze will not be clear. Let the sugar mixture bubble until it starts to turn faintly golden around the edges of the pan. Stir in the sesame seeds and reduce the heat to as low as possible. Or remove the pan from the heat, replacing it from time to time if the sugar begins to harden before the apples have been dipped.

While you are preparing the glaze, heat the peanut oil in a large heavy-based saucepan over medium heat – ideally the oil for deep-frying and the sugar glaze should be ready at the same time. Drop pieces of apple into the batter, one at a time, turning to coat, then use chopsticks to gently lower them into the hot oil. Deep-fry until the batter is golden, then lift out with a slotted spoon and put straight into the saucepan containing the hot glaze, turning to coat. Lift out, then drop straight into a bowl containing cold water and ice cubes. The glaze will harden and become brittle almost at once. Lift them out quickly and put on a lightly oiled serving plate. Serve and eat as soon as possible. If left to stand too long the glaze will melt and the batter will become leathery.

Agar-Agar Jelly

Serves: 6

1 tablespoon agar-agar powder

220 g (8 oz/1 cup) sugar

3–4 drops red food colouring

3–4 drops rosewater

½ teaspoon natural vanilla extract

3–4 drops green food colouring

3–4 drops natural almond extract

Put 1.5 litres (51 fl oz/6 cups) water into a saucepan with the agar-agar powder and bring to the boil. Boil for about 5–10 minutes, or until the agar-agar dissolves. Add the sugar and stir until it dissolves. Remove from the heat.

Pour 500 ml (17 fl oz/2 cups) of the liquid into a pitcher (reserving the remaining liquid in the warm pan). Colour the liquid pink with the red food colouring and add the rosewater to flavour. Pour into a glass serving bowl rinsed with cold water and refrigerate for a few minutes to set.

As soon as the first layer sets pour 500 ml (17 fl oz/2 cups) of the warm liquid into the pitcher and flavour with the vanilla extract. Pour gently over the first pink layer of jelly and refrigerate until set.

Put the remaining liquid into the pitcher, colour it pale green with the green food colouring and add the almond extract for flavour. Spoon over the first 2 layers, then refrigerate until ready to serve.

Silver Fungus in Sweet Soup

Serves: 6

3 tablespoons silver fungus (glossary)

120 g (4½ oz/¾ cup) crushed rock sugar or white sugar

670 g (1½ lb) tinned longans, lychees or palm seeds in syrup

12 ice cubes

Soak the silver fungus in hot water for 10 minutes, then drain well.

Put the silver fungus into a saucepan with the sugar and 500 ml (17 fl oz/2 cups) water and bring to the boil, stirring until the sugar has dissolved. Cover and simmer for 10 minutes. Remove from the heat and allow to cool, then refrigerate until well chilled.

Before serving, combine the fruit and chilled syrup in a serving bowl and add the ice cubes. Alternatively, you can serve warm or at room temperature and omit the ice cubes.

Glossary
and
Index

Agar-agar

A setting agent obtained from seaweed, agar-agar is widely used in Asia, as it sets without refrigeration. It is sold in sachets in powder form and is available from Asian grocery stores and health food stores. It is also sold in strands, though they are less obtainable and slower to dissolve. Also known as: *kyauk kyaw* (Burma), *dai choy goh* (China), *kanten* (Japan), *gulaman* (Philippines), *chun chow* (Sri Lanka), *woon* (Thailand), *rau cau* (Vietnam).

Aromatic ginger

See galangal, lesser.

Bamboo shoots

Sold in tins and jars, either water-packed, pickled or braised. Unless otherwise stated, the recipes in this book use the water-packed variety. If using the tinned variety, store left-over bamboo shoots in a bowl of fresh water in the refrigerator, changing the water daily for up to 10 days. Winter bamboo shoots are much smaller and more tender, and are called for in certain recipes. However, if they are not available, use the larger variety. Also known as: *wah-bho-khmyit* (Burma), *tumpeang* (Cambodia), *suehn* (China), *rebung* (Indonesia), *takenoko* (Japan), *rebong* (Malaysia), *labong* (Philippines), *normai* (Thailand), *mang* (Vietnam).

Barbecue (char siu) sauce

A reddish sauce, *char siu* is very salty and at the same time heavily sweetened. Use as a dip or as an ingredient in barbecue marinades. Keeps indefinitely in an airtight jar.

Bitter melon (gourd)

Botanical name: *Momordica charantia*
Known variously as bitter melon, bitter gourd, bitter cucumber and balsam pear, this vaguely reptilian-looking vegetable with a warty green exterior should be purchased while young and shiny-skinned. Do not store more than a day or two and even then in the refrigerator, or it will continue to mature. Over-ripe specimens will yellow and their seeds will become very hard. Cultures all over Asia believe this vegetable has powerful medicinal benefits. Also known as: *kyethinkhathee* (Burma), *fu gwa, foo kwa* (China), *karela* (India), *pare, peria* (Indonesia), *niga-uri* (Japan), *maha* (Laos), *peria* (Malaysia), *ampalaya* (Philippines), *karavila* (Sri Lanka), *bai mara* (Thailand), *kho qua* (Vietnam).

Black beans, salted

Made from soy beans, heavily salted and sold in tins and jars. Rinse before using to avoid over-salting recipes. Substitute extra soy sauce for flavour, though not for appearance. Store in an airtight jar in the refrigerator after opening – it will keep for 6 months or longer. Pour a little peanut oil over it if the top seems to dry out. Also known as: *dow see* (China).

Candlenuts

Botanical name: *Aleurites moluccana*
A hard oily nut used to flavour and thicken Indonesian and Malaysian curries. The name arises because the nuts, when threaded on the mid-rib of a palm leaf, are used as a primitive candle. Because of the high oil content, store in the freezer to prevent rancidity. Use Brazil nuts or macadamia nuts as a substitute, though their flavour is sweeter than that of the candlenut. Also known as: *kyainthee* (Burma), *kemiri* (Indonesia), *buah keras* (Malaysia), *lumbang bato* (Philippines), *kekuna, tel kekuna* (Sri Lanka).

Cardamom

Botanical name: *Elettaria cardamomum*
Next to saffron, cardamom is the world's most expensive spice. Cardamoms grow mainly in India and Sri Lanka, and are the seed pods of a member of the ginger family. The dried seed pods are either pale green or brown, according to variety; sometimes they are bleached white. They are added, either whole or bruised, to pilaus and other rice dishes, spiced curries and other preparations or sweets. When ground cardamom is called for, the seed pods are opened and discarded and only the small black or brown seeds are ground. For full flavour, it is best to grind them just before using. If you cannot buy a high-quality ground cardamom, crush the seeds using a mortar and pestle or spice mill, as required. Also known as: *phalazee* (Burma), *illaichi* (India), *kapulaga* (Indonesia), *buah pelaga* (Malaysia), *enasal* (Sri Lanka), *kravan* (Thailand).

Cellophane (bean thread) noodles

These are fine, translucent noodles made from the starch of green mung beans. The noodles may be soaked in hot water before use, or may require boiling according to the texture required. They can also be deep-fried straight from the packet, generally when used as a garnish or to provide a background for other foods. Also known as: *kyazan* (Burma), *mee sooer* (Cambodia), *bi fun, ning fun, sai fun, fun see* (China), *sotanghoon* (Indonesia), *harusame* (Japan), *sohoon, tunghoon* (Malaysia), *sotanghon* (Philippines), *woon sen* (Thailand), *búng u, mien* (Vietnam).

Chilli powder

Asian chilli powder is made from ground chillies. It is much hotter than the Mexican-style chilli powder, which is mostly ground cumin. You may be able to find ground Kashmiri chillies, which are a brighter red colour and not as hot as other ground chillies.

Chillies, bird's eye

Very small, very hot chillies. Used mainly in pickles, though in some cases added to food when a very hot flavour is required (as in Thai food). Treat with caution and wear disposable gloves when handling seeds. As with all chillies, the seeds and membrane contain the highest concentration of volatile oil. Also known as: *cili padi* (Malaysia), *siling labuyo* (Philippines), *kochchi miris* (Sri Lanka), *prik kee noo suan* (Thailand).

Chillies, green and red

Botanical name: *Capsicum* spp.
Chillies mature from green to red, becoming hotter as they mature. Both varieties are used fresh for flavouring, either whole or finely chopped, sliced as a garnish or ground into sambals. The seeds, which are the hottest parts, are usually (though not always) removed. Larger varieties tend to be milder than the small varieties. See page 10 for handling. Dried red chillies are found in packets in Asian grocery stores – the medium- to large-sized chillies are best for most recipes in this book.

Chinese five-spice

Essential in Chinese cooking, this reddish-brown powder is a combination of ground star anise, fennel, cinnamon, cloves and sichuan pepper. Also known as: *heung new fun, hung liu, ngung heung fun* (China).

Chinese sausages (lap cheong)

These dried sausages are filled only with spiced lean and fat pork. Steam for 10–15 minutes until soft and plump and the fat is translucent. Cut into thin slices to serve, or include in other dishes. They have a sweet, lightly scented flavour that can be an acquired taste.

Cinnamon

Botanical name: *Cinnamomum zeylanicum* and *verum*
True cinnamon is native to Sri Lanka. Buy cinnamon sticks or quills rather than the ground spice, which loses its flavour when stored too long. It is used in both sweet and savoury dishes. Cassia, which is grown in India, Indonesia and Burma, is similar. It is much stronger in flavour, and is cheaper, but it lacks the delicacy of cinnamon. The leaves and buds of the cassia tree have a flavour similar to the bark and are also used for flavouring food. For sweet dishes, use true cinnamon. Cassia bark is much thicker because the corky layer is left on. Also known as: *thit-ja-boh-guak* (Burma), *darchini* (India), *kayu manis* (Malaysia and Indonesia), *kurundu* (Sri Lanka), *op chery* (Thailand), *que* (Vietnam).

Cloves

Botanical name: *Syzygium aromaticum, Eugenia aromatica* and *E. caryophyllus*
Cloves are the dried flower buds of an evergreen tropical tree native to Southeast Asia. They were used in China more than 2000 years ago, and were also used by the Romans. Oil of cloves contains phenol, a powerful antiseptic that discourages putrefaction, and the clove is hence one of the spices that helps preserve food. Also known as: *ley-nyin-bwint* (Burma), *laung* (India), *cengkeh* (Indonesia), *bunga cingkeh* (Malaysia), *karabu* (Sri Lanka), *kaan ploo* (Thailand).

Coconut milk

This is not the water inside the nut, as is commonly believed, but the creamy liquid extracted from the grated flesh of fresh coconuts or from desiccated or shredded coconut (pages 8–9). When coconut milk is called for, especially in sweet dishes, do make an effort to use it, for its flavour cannot be duplicated by using any other kind of milk. Tinned and Tetra Pak coconut milk saves time and effort, although be warned that some brands are far better than others so try a few until you find one that appeals. Low-fat coconut milk is an unappealing substitute.

Coriander (cilantro)

Botanical name: *Coriandrum sativum*
All parts of the coriander (cilantro) plant are used in Asian cooking. The dried seed is the main ingredient in curry powder, and although not hot it has a fragrance that makes it an essential part of a curry blend. The fresh coriander herb is also known as cilantro or Chinese parsley in other parts of the world. It is indispensable in Burma, Thailand, Vietnam, Cambodia, India and China where it is also called 'fragrant green'. Also known as: *nannamzee* (seed), *nannambin* (leaves) (Burma), *chee van soy* (Cambodia), *yuen sai* (China), *dhania* (seed), *dhania pattar,* *dhania sabz* (leaves) (India), *phak hom pom* (Laos), *ketumbar* (seeds), *daun ketumbar* (leaves) (Malaysia), *kinchay* (Philippines), *kottamalli* (seed), *kottamalli kolle* (leaves) (Sri Lanka), *pak chee* (Thailand), *ngò, rau mùi* (Vietnam).

Cumin

Botanical name: *Cuminum cyminum*
Cumin is, with coriander, the most essential ingredient in prepared curry powders. It is available as seed, or ground. There may be some confusion between cumin and caraway seeds because they are similar in appearance, but the flavours are completely different and one cannot replace the other in recipes. Also known as: *ma-ch'in* (China), *sufaid zeera* (white cumin), *zeera, jeera* (India), *jinten* (Indonesia), *kumin* (Japan), *jintan puteh* (Malaysia), *sududuru* (Sri Lanka), *yira* (Thailand).

Curry leaves

Botanical name: *Murraya koenigii*
Sold fresh or dried, they are as important to curries as bay leaves are to stews, but never try to substitute one for the other. The tree is native to Asia, the leaves are small, pointed and shiny, growing in opposing pairs along a central stalk. Although they keep their flavour well when dried or frozen, they are found in such abundance in Asia that they are generally used fresh. The tree is easy to grow from seed even in a temperate climate. The leaves are fried in oil until crisp at the start of preparing a curry. Dried curry leaves can be pulverised using a mortar and pestle; and the powdered leaves can be used in marinades and omelettes. Also known as: *pyi-naw-thein* (Burma), *kitha neem, katnim, karipattar, karuvepila* (India), *daun kari, karupillay* (Malaysia), *karapincha* (Sri Lanka).

Daikon

Botanical name: *Raphanus sativus*
Daikon (white radish) is a very large white radish most popularly known by its Japanese name and it is about 30–38 cm (12–15¼ in) long with a mild flavour. It is sold in Asian grocery stores and some large greengrocers and supermarkets. Substitute white turnip if not available. Also known as: *loh hahk* (China), *muuli* (India), *lobak* (Indonesia and Malaysia), *mu (moo)* (Korea), *labanos* (Philippines), *rabu* (Sri Lanka), *phakkat-hua* (Thailand), *cù cùi trng* (Vietnam).

Daun pandan

See pandanus or screwpine.

Daun salam

An aromatic leaf used in Indonesian cooking, it is larger than the curry leaf used in India and Sri Lanka, but has a slightly cinnamon flavour. There is no substitute.

Dried fish (sprats)

Salting and drying fish is a common way of preserving fish throughout Asia. Some are small, such as tiny sprats or anchovies. These tiny sprats or anchovies should be rinsed before use. Avoid soaking them, or they will not retain their crispness when fried. Dry on paper towel before frying. Larger salted and dried fish, such as *karavadu*, are used in main dishes. Also known as: *nga chauk* (Burma), *nethali* (India), *ikan bilis* (Indonesia and Malaysia), *dilis* (Philippines), *haal masso* (Sri Lanka), *plasroi* (Thailand).

Fennel
Botanical name: *Foeniculum vulgare*
Sometimes known as 'sweet cumin' or 'large cumin', because of its similar-shaped seeds, it is a member of the same botanical family and is used in Sri Lankan curries (but in much smaller quantities than true cumin). It is available in ground or seed form. Substitute an equal amount of aniseed. Also known as: *samouk-saba* (Burma), *sonf* (India), *adas* (Indonesia), *jintan manis* (Malaysia), *maduru* (Sri Lanka), *yira* (Thailand).

Fenugreek
Botanical name: *Trigonella foenum-graecum*
These small, flat, squarish, brownish-beige seeds are essential in curries, but because they have a slightly bitter flavour they must be used in the stated quantities. They are especially good in fish and seafood curries, where the whole seeds are gently fried at the start of cooking; they are also ground and added to curry powders. The green leaves are used in Indian cooking and, when spiced, the bitter taste is quite piquant and acceptable. The plant is easy to grow and, when at the two-leaf stage, the sprouts make a tangy addition to salads. Also known as: *methi* (India), *alba* (Malaysia), *uluhaal* (Sri Lanka).

Fish cakes
Both Chinese-style fish cakes and Japanese-style fish cakes are sold ready to use in most Asian grocery stores. They can be kept for a few days if refrigerated, and need no further cooking apart from heating through.

Fish sauce
A thin, salty, brown sauce used in Southeast Asian cooking to bring out the flavour in other foods. A small variety of fish is packed in wooden barrels with salt, and the liquid that runs off is the 'fish sauce'. There are different grades of fish sauce, the Vietnamese version being darker and having a more pronounced fish flavour than the others. Also known as: *ngan-pya-ye* (Burma), *tuck trey* (Cambodia), *nam pa* (Laos), *patis* (Philippines), *nam pla* (Thailand), *nuoc nam* (Vietnam).

Galangal, greater
Botanical name: *Alpinia galanga*
A rhizome, like ginger, galangal has thin brown skin and the flesh is creamy white. As it ages, galangal becomes woody and can be very tough to cut and difficult to grind. Scrape off the skin and chop the root finely before pounding or grinding in spice pastes. Slices may be simmered in soups and curries for extra flavour. The young rhizome is most attractive with smooth skin blushing pink. The greater galangal is more extensively used in Southeast Asian cooking than lesser galangal, and is more delicate in flavour, although if absent from a dish, it will be missed. Also known as: *pa-de-gaw-gyi* (Burma), *romdaeng* (Cambodia), *gao liang jiang, lam kieu, lam keong* (China), *kulanjan, kosht-kulinjan, pera-rattai* (India), *laos* (Indonesia), *lengkuas* (Malaysia), *kha* (Thailand and Laos), *riêng* (Vietnam). *See also galangal, lesser (aromatic ginger).*

Galangal, lesser (aromatic ginger)
Botanical name: *Kaempferia pandurata, Alpinia officinarum*
Also known as 'aromatic ginger', this member of the ginger family cannot be used as a substitute for ginger or vice versa. It is used only in certain dishes and gives a pronounced aromatic flavour. When available fresh, it is sliced or pounded to a pulp; but outside of Asia it is usually sold dried, and the hard round slices must be pounded using a mortar and pestle or pulverised in a food processor before use. In some spice ranges it is sold in powdered form as kencur powder. The plant is native to southern China and has been used for centuries in medicinal herbal mixtures, but it is not used in Chinese cooking. Also known as: *sa leung geung, sha geung fun* (China), *kencur* (Indonesia), *zeodary* or *kencur* (Malaysia), *ingurupiyali* (Sri Lanka), *krachai* (Thailand).

Ghee (clarified butter)
Sold in tins, ghee is pure butterfat without any of the milk solids. It can be heated to much higher temperatures than butter without burning, and imparts a distinctive flavour when used as a cooking medium.

Glutinous rice
Botanical name: *Oryza sativa* var. *glutinosa* and *glutinosa*
Although also known as sticky rice, because of its sticky consistency, it actually contains no gluten. Cooked both as whole grains, milled and unmilled (with bran removed or intact), as well as ground into flour. The purple and black varieties are different strains. Mostly used to make sweets except in Laos, where it is eaten in place of ordinary rice. Also known as: *kao hnyin* (Burma), *bai dow map* (Cambodia), *nuomi* (China), *ketan* (Indonesia), *mochigome* (Japan), *chapssal* (Korea), *khao niao* (Laos and Thailand), *pulot* (Malaysia), *malagkit* (Philippines), *go np* (Vietnam).

Gourd, bitter
See bitter melon.

Ground rice
See rice, ground.

Hoisin sauce
A sweet, spicy, reddish-brown sauce of thick pouring consistency made from soy beans, garlic and spices. Used in barbecued pork dishes and as a dip. Keeps indefinitely in an airtight jar.

Jicama
See yam bean.

Kecap manis
See soy sauce.

Kencur (aromatic ginger) powder
See galangal, lesser.

Laos (dried galangal) powder
Botanical name: *Alpinia galanga*
A very delicate spice, sold in powder form, *laos* is the ground, dried root of the 'greater galangal'. The fresh or bottled rhizome will have more impact, but the ground spice can add an intriguing note to curries and dishes requiring longer cooking. *See galangal, greater.*

Lemongrass

Botanical name: *Cymbopogon citratus*

This aromatic Asian plant is a tall grass with sharp-edged leaves that multiply into clumps. The whitish, slightly bulbous base is used to impart a lemony flavour to curries, salads and soups. Cut just one stem with a sharp knife, close to the root, and use about 10–12 cm (4–4¾ in) of the stalk from the base, discarding the leaves. If you have to use dried lemongrass, about 12 strips dried are equal to 1 fresh stem; although 2–3 strips of very thinly peeled lemon zest will do just as well. Dried ground lemongrass is known as sereh powder in Indonesia. Also known as: *zabalin* (Burma), *kreung, bai mak nao* (Cambodia), *heung masu tso* (China), *sera* (India and Sri Lanka), *sereh* (Indonesia), *remon-sou* (Japan), *serai* (Malaysia), *takrai* (Thailand), *xa* (Vietnam).

Mace

Botanical name: *Myristica fragrans*

Mace is part of the nutmeg, a fruit that looks like an apricot and grows on tall tropical trees. When ripe, the fruit splits to reveal the aril, lacy and bright scarlet, surrounding the shell of the seed; the dried aril is mace and the kernel is nutmeg. Mace has a flavour similar to nutmeg but more delicate, and it is sometimes used in meat or fish curries, especially in Sri Lanka, although its main use in Asia is medicinal (a few blades of mace steeped in hot water, the water then being taken to combat nausea and diarrhoea). Also known as: *javatri* (India), *wasa-vasi* (Sri Lanka).

Melinjo nut

Botanical name: *Gnetum gnemon*

The kernel of the small oval fruits of the gnemon tree, the boiled and dried seeds are then flattened and deep-fried in hot oil to make delicious wafers. Sometimes labelled 'bitter nut crackers', they make a great snack or appetiser and are sometimes used to garnish Indonesian dishes. Also known as: *belinjo* (Indonesia).

Miso

A paste made from cooked, fermented soy beans. There are various types: white, red, brownish and beige – with white and red being the main ones. There are also varying degrees of saltiness, so make sure you allow for it. Japanese thick soups are mostly based on miso stirred into dashi, the usual proportion being 1 tablespoon to 250 ml (8½ fl oz/1 cup) of stock. There is also a yellow bean paste used in Singapore and Indonesia called *taucheo*. *See salted soy beans (taucheo)*.

Mushrooms, shiitake (dried)

Botanical name: *Lentinus edodes*

Also known as 'fragrant mushrooms', the flavour of these mushrooms is quite individual. They are expensive but give an incomparable flavour. Soak for 20–30 minutes before using. The stems are usually discarded and only the caps used. There is no substitute. Also known as: *hmo chauk* (Burma), *doong gwoo, leong goo* (China), *cindauwan* (Malaysia), *kabuteng shiitakena pinatuyo* (Philippines), *hed hom* (Thailand), *khô nm shiitake, nm ro'm khô* (Vietnam).

Mustard cabbage (gai choy)

Botanical name: *Brassica juncea*

Mustard cabbage (gai choy), or Sichuan vegetable, is often preserved in brine, with chilli added. It can be used as a relish, or included in dishes requiring piquancy and tang. Sold in tins. Also known as: *dai gai choy, jook gai choy* (China), *sarson* (India), *sawi hijau* (Indonesia), *takana, karashi-na* (Japan), *mustasa* (Philippines), *abba kolle* (Sri Lanka), *phakkat khieo* (Thailand), *rau cai* (Vietnam).

Nutmeg

Botanical name: *Myristica fragrans*

Not widely used as a curry spice, but used to flavour some sweets and cakes, and sometimes used in garam masala. For maximum flavour, always grate finely just before using. Use sparingly, as large quantities (more than one whole nut) can be poisonous. Also known as: *zalipho thi* (Burma), *tau kau* (China), *jaiphal* (India), *pala* (Indonesia), *buah pala* (Malaysia), *sadikka* (Sri Lanka).

Oyster sauce

Adds delicate flavour to all kinds of dishes. Made from oysters cooked in soy sauce and brine, this thick brown sauce can be kept indefinitely in the refrigerator. Also known as: *ho yu* (China).

Palm sugar (jaggery)

This strong-flavoured dark sugar is obtained from the sap of coconut palms and Palmyrah palms. The sap is boiled down until it crystallises, and the sugar is usually sold in round, flat cakes or two hemispheres put together to form a ball and wrapped in dried leaves. Substitute black sugar, an unrefined, sticky sugar sold in health food stores, or use refined dark brown sugar sold at supermarkets. Thai recipes generally call for pale palm sugar, while Malaysian, Indonesian and Sri Lankan recipes favour dark palm sugar. Also known as: *jaggery, tanyet* (Burma), *skor tnowth* (Cambodia), *gur, jaggery* (India), *gula aren, gula jawa* (Indonesia), *gula Melaka* (Malaysia), *jaggery, hakuru* (Sri Lanka), *nam taan pep, nam taan bik, nam taan mapraow* (Thailand).

Pandanus or screwpine

Botanical name: *Pandanus latifolia*

Used as a flavouring in rice and curries in Sri Lanka, to wrap chicken for grilling or deep-frying in Thailand and Cambodia and as a flavouring and colouring agent in Malay and Indonesian sweets. The long, flat, green leaves are either crushed or boiled to yield up their flavour and colour. In Malaysia and Indonesia especially, the flavour is as popular as vanilla is in the West. It is available fresh and frozen in Asian grocery stores and increasingly common in good greengrocers. Also known as: *slok toey* (Cambodia), *daun pandan* (Indonesia and Malaysia), *rampe* (Sri Lanka), *bai toey* (Thailand).

Peanut oil

A traditional cooking medium in Chinese and Southeast Asian countries. Asian unrefined peanut oil is highly flavoured and more expensive than the refined peanut oil found in Western supermarkets. It has a high smoking point and adds a distinctive flavour to stir-fries. Refined peanut oil is ideal for deep-frying. Take all the usual precautions where peanuts are concerned and avoid it if cooking for anyone with nut sensitivities. Use olive oil flavoured with a little sesame oil as an alternative.

Plum sauce

A spicy, sweet Chinese sauce made from plums, chillies, vinegar, spices and sugar. Use as a dip. It keeps indefinitely in an airtight jar.

Prawn powder, dried
Finely shredded dried prawns (shrimp), sold in packets at speciality food stores and Asian grocery stores.

Red asian shallots
Botanical name: *Allium ascalonicum*
Shallots are small, purplish onions with red-brown skin. Like garlic, they grow in a cluster and resemble garlic cloves in shape. The name 'shallots' in Australia is generally (and incorrectly) given to spring onions in some states.

Red food colouring powder
A brilliant red powder sold in Chinese grocery stores and used very sparingly to give the distinctive colour seen in barbecued pork. Substitute a bright red liquid food colouring if unavailable. Powdered annatto seeds or paprika may be substituted, although the red they produce is not nearly as vivid.

Rice, ground
This can be bought at supermarkets and health food stores. It is slightly more granular than rice flour. It gives a crisper texture when used in batters.

Rice vermicelli (rice-stick) noodles
These are very fine rice flour noodles sold in Chinese grocery stores. Soaking in hot water for 10 minutes prepares them sufficiently for most recipes, but in some cases they may need boiling for 1–2 minutes. When deep-fried they swell up and turn white. For a crisp result, fry them straight from the packet without soaking. Also known as: *mee sooer* (Cambodia), *mei fun* (China), *beehoon, meehoon* (Malaysia), *sen mee* (Thailand), *bún, lúa min* (Vietnam).

Rosewater
A favourite flavouring in Indian and Persian sweets, rosewater is the diluted essence extracted from rose petals by steam distillation. It is essential in many desserts, and is also used in biriani. If you substitute rose essence or concentrate, be careful not to over-flavour and be sure to count the drops. However, with rosewater a 1 tablespoon-measure can safely be used. Buy rosewater from chemists or from shops specialising in Asian or Middle Eastern ingredients.

Roti flour
Creamy in colour and slightly granular in texture, this is ideal flour for all unleavened breads; unlike atta flour, it is not made from the whole wheat grain but instead the polished or milled grain. Sold at some health food stores and Chinese grocery stores as well as Indian grocery stores.

Salted soy beans (taucheo)
An Indonesian or Malaysian fermented soy bean sauce. The beans may be whole, but are very soft and easy to mash. Yellow bean sauce is a smooth version. Thai soy bean paste is a suitable substitute. Also sold as *tauco* and *tauceo*.

Sambal bajak
A combination of chillies and spices used as an accompaniment to rice and curry meals. Sold in Asian grocery stores. Some Dutch-manufactured brands still use the old Dutch-Indonesian spelling, *sambal badjak*.

Sambal ulek
A combination of chillies and salt, used in cooking or as an accompaniment. The old Dutch-Indonesian spelling, still seen on some labels, is *sambal oelek*.

Sesame oil
The sesame oil used in Chinese cooking is extracted from toasted sesame seeds and gives a totally different flavour from the lighter-coloured sesame oil sold in health food stores. For the recipes in this book, buy sesame oil from Asian grocery stores. Use the oil in small quantities for flavouring, not as a cooking medium. Also known as: *hnan zi* (Burma), *ma yau* (China), *gingelly, til ka tel* (India), *goma abura* (Japan), *chan keh room* (Korea), *minyak bijan* (Malaysia), *thala tel* (Sri Lanka), *dau me* (Vietnam).

Sesame seeds
Used mostly in Korean, Chinese and Japanese food, and in sweets in other Southeast Asian countries. Black sesame, another variety known as *hak chih mah* (China) or *kuro goma* (Japan), is mainly used in the Chinese dessert, toffee apples, and as a flavouring (gomashio) mixed with salt in Japanese food. Also known as: *hnan si* (Burma), *til, gingelly* (India), *wijen* (Indonesia), *keh* (Korea), *bijan* (Malaysia), *linga* (Philippines), *thala* (Sri Lanka), *nga dee la* (Thailand), *me* (Vietnam).

Shrimp paste, dried
Commercially sold as blacan, blachan or belacan, this is a pungent paste made from prawns (shrimp), and used in many Southeast Asian recipes. It is sold in tins, flat slabs or blocks and will keep indefinitely. If stored in an airtight jar it will, like a genie in a bottle, perform its magic when required without obtruding on the kitchen at other times! It does not need refrigeration. Also known as: *ngapi* (Burma), *trasi* (Indonesia), *blacan* (Malaysia), *kapi* (Thailand), *mam tom* (Vietnam).

Shrimp sauce
Although sometimes distributed as *bagoong* (Philippines) or *petis* (Indonesia), this is sold at Asian grocery stores as 'shrimp sauce' or 'shrimp paste'. Thick and greyish in colour, with a powerful odour, it is one of the essential ingredients in the food of Southeast Asia. Substitute dried shrimp paste (blacan) or anchovy sauce.

Silver fungus
Also known as 'white wood fungus', this is so rare and expensive that it is used only in special festive dishes. Almost flavourless, it is prized for its crunchy texture and pretty appearance, and is also a 'prestige' food used to honour special guests. It is sold dried by the gram, or in tins cooked in a sweet syrup. However, the homemade version is infinitely preferable to the tinned silver fungus, which loses its texture through processing. Silver fungus is said to be very beneficial to pregnant women. Also known as: *sit gnee* (China), *shiro kikurage* (Japan), *cendawan jelly puteh* (Malaysia).

Soy sauce
Indispensable in Asian cooking, this versatile sauce enhances the flavour of every basic ingredient in a dish. Different grades are available. Chinese cooking uses light soy and dark soy. The light soy is used with chicken or seafoods, or in soups where the delicate colour of the dish must be retained. Always use shoyu

(Japanese soy sauce) in Japanese cooking. In Indonesia, *kecap manis*, a thick, dark, sweetened soy, is often used. As a substitute, use dark Chinese soy with black or brown sugar added in the proportions given in recipes. All types of soy sauce keep indefinitely without refrigeration.

Spring roll pastry
Thin, white sheets of pliable pastry sold in plastic packets and kept frozen. Thaw and peel off one at a time (unused wrappers can be re-frozen). Large wrappers of the won ton type cannot be substituted.

Star anise
Botanical name: *Illicium verum*
The dried, star-shaped fruit of an evergreen tree native to China and Vietnam, it usually consists of eight segments or points. It is essential in Chinese cooking and is one of the key flavours in the stock for the Vietnamese rice noodle soup, *pho*. Also known as: *baht gok* (China), *badian* (India), *bunga lawang* (Indonesia and Malaysia), *poy kak bua* (Thailand), *hoi* (Vietnam).

Tamarind
Botanical name: *Tamarindus indica*
The tamarind is a sour-tasting fruit of a large tropical tree. It is shaped like a large broad (fava) bean and has a brittle brown shell, inside which are shiny dark seeds covered with tangy brown flesh. Tamarind is dried into a pulp and sold in packets, as well as diluted with water and sold as a purée. These can vary in concentration. The pulp needs to be soaked first in hot water, then squeezed until it breaks up and dissolves. It needs to be strained before using. May be substituted with lemon juice. Also known as: *ma-gyi-thi* (Burma), *ampil tum* (ripe), *ampil kheei* (green) (Cambodia), *imli* (India), *mal kham* (Laos), *asam* (Malaysia and Indonesia), *sampalok* (Philippines), *siyambala* (Sri Lanka), *som ma kham* (Thailand), *me* (Vietnam).

Taucheo
See salted soy beans.

Tofu
There is an abundance of varieties of this versatile soy product available. Fresh tofu, or bean curd, is found in the refrigerator section of Asian grocery stores and most large supermarkets. It comes in many forms: silken, soft or firm. Silken tofu is sweeter and more delicate than firm tofu, with a different texture and flavour. Once opened, tofu will keep for 2–3 days in the refrigerator if immersed in cold water that is changed daily. Dried tofu is sold in flat sheets or rounded sticks and needs no refrigeration. It has to be soaked before use – the sticks need longer soaking and cooking. Deep-fried tofu puffs are also available. Red tofu is much more pungent than fresh tofu, and has a flavour like smelly cheese. It is sold in bottles and used in certain sauces. Also known as: *dow foo, doufu, doufu-ru* (China), *tahu* (Indonesia), *doufu-kan, abura-age, yuba* (Japan), *taukwa* (Malaysia), *tojo, tokua* (Philippines), *tao hu, forng tao hu* (Thailand), *dau hu* (Vietnam).

Turmeric
Botanical name: *Curcuma longa*
A rhizome of the ginger family, turmeric, with its orange-yellow colour, is a mainstay of commercial curry powders. Though often called Indian saffron, it should never be confused with true saffron and the two may not be used interchangeably. Also known as: *fa nwin, sa nwin* (Burma), *romiet* (Cambodia), *wong geung fun* (China), *haldi* (India), *kunyit* (Indonesia), *ukon* (Japan), *kunyit* (Malaysia), *dilau* (Philippines), *kaha* (Sri Lanka), *khamin* (Thailand), *cú nghê, ngh* (Vietnam).

Water chestnuts
Botanical name: *Eliocharis dulcis*
Used mainly for their texture in Asian cooking. Sometimes available fresh, their brownish black skin must be peeled away with a sharp knife, leaving the crisp, slightly sweet white kernel. They are also available in tins, already peeled and in some instances sliced. After opening, store in water in the refrigerator for 7–10 days, changing the water daily. Yam bean (jicama) may be substituted if water chestnut is unavailable. Dried, powdered water chestnut starch is used as an alternative to cornflour (cornstarch) for coating delicate meat such as chicken breast when deep-frying, as it helps lock in the juices. Also known as: *ye thit eir thee* (Burma), *mah tai* (China), *pani phul* (India), *tike* (Indonesia), *kuwai, kurogu-wai* (Japan), *apulid* (Philippines), *haeo-song krathiem, haeo cheen* (Thailand), *go nung* (Vietnam).

Winter bamboo shoots
See bamboo shoots.

Wood ear fungus
Botanical name: *Auricalaria polytricha*
Also known as black fungus, cloud ear fungus, tree ear fungus, mouse ear or jelly mushroom, wood ear fungus is sold by weight, and in its dry state looks like greyish black pieces of torn paper. Soaked in hot water for 10 minutes, it swells to translucent brown shapes like curved clouds or a rather prettily shaped ear – hence the name 'wood ear fungus'. With its flavourless resilience it is a perfect example of a texture ingredient, adding no taste of its own but taking on subtle flavours from the foods with which it is combined. Cook for only 1–2 minutes. Also known as: *kyet neywet* (Burma), *wun yee* (China), *kuping jamu* (Indonesia), *kikurage* (Japan), *kuping tikus* (Malaysia), *hed hunu* (Thailand).

Yam bean (jicama)
Botanical name: *Pachyrhizus erosus* and *P. angulatus*
Curiously, the growers' notes say this plant of the legume family, which bears seed pods, has tubers which may be boiled like a potato. That is the last thing I would use them for. The main appeal of yam bean is the sweet crisp crunch of its white, uncooked flesh. I would recommend using it raw, peeled and sliced or diced, in salads or sweets; or even lightly cooked in stir-fries, where it might retain some of its characteristic crunch. Yam beans are a very acceptable substitute for water chestnuts, when they are unavailable. Also known as: *saa got, dou-su* (China), *sankalu* (India), *bengkowang* (Indonesia), *kuzu-imu* (Japan), *bangkwang, singkwang* (Malaysia), *singkamas* (Philippines), *man kaew* (Thailand), *cu san* (Vietnam).

INDEX

A

abon daging 68
acar ikan 134
acar kuning 152
accompaniments
  Chilli-fried cauliflower 150
  Coconut wafers 30
  Crisp spiced coconut with peanuts 111
  Crisp spiced coconut with peanuts (quick
    method) 111
  Eggs in chilli sauce 62
  Eggs in soy sauce 63
  Fried bananas 106
  Fried melinjo nut wafers 106
  Fried onion flakes 105
  Marbled eggs 104
  Peanut wafers 30
  Prawn crisps 31
  Spicy fruit salad 108
  Vegetable pickle 152
  see also sambals; sauces
agar-agar 206
Agar-agar jelly 204
Almond biscuits 201
aromatic ginger 208
asam babi goreng 78
ayam bali 60
ayam goreng asam 58
ayam goreng jawa 56
ayam lemak 138
ayam panggang 54
ayam panggang pedis 60
ayam petis 57

B

Baked fish 43
Balinese-style beef strips 66
Balinese-style fish 38
Balinese-style fried chicken 60
bamboo shoots 206
  Chicken and bamboo shoot curry 139
  Fresh spring rolls 174
banana leaves 25, 43
  Fish grilled in banana leaves 37
bananas, Fried 106
barbecue (char siu) sauce 206
Barbecue-style pork with black beans 194
bawang goreng 105
bean sprouts
  Hokkien mee soup 170
  Stir-fried prawns with bean sprouts and
    snow peas 176
  Tofu and bean sprouts 148
bean thread/starch noodles 12
beans
  Barbecue-style pork with black beans 194

Bean sayur 93
Fish in brown bean sauce with stir-fried
  vegetables 36
Green bean sambal 103
Prawns in chilli bean sauce 182
salted black beans 206
yam bean (jicama) 211
beef
  Balinese-style beef strips 66
  Beef cooked in soy sauce 73
  Beef satay 191
  Beef in soy sauce and chillies 76
  Beef spareribs special 67
  Dried spiced meat 77
  Dry-fried beef curry 72
  Eastern-style croquettes 189
  Javanese-style fried meatballs 80
  Malay beef satay 144
  Meat and coconut patties 82
  Semarang-style sliced beef 66
  Shredded crisp-fried meat 68
  Spicy beef satay 84
bird's eye chillies 50, 206
biscuits, Almond 201
bitter melon (gourd) 206

C

cabbage
  mustard cabbage (chai goy) 209
  Spicy cabbage in coconut milk 88
  Spring rolls 171
cake: Many layered spice cake 114
candlenuts 206
cardamom 206
cauliflower, Chilli-fried 150
cellophane (bean thread) noodles 12, 206
chai goy 209
char kway teow 122
chatties 161
chee cheong fun 165
chicken
  Balinese-style fried chicken 60
  Bean sayur 93
  Chicken and bamboo shoot curry 139
  Chicken in coconut milk (Indonesian) 53
  Chicken in coconut milk (Malaysian) 140
  Chicken curry with toasted coconut 137
  Chicken grilled on skewers 61
  Chicken with shrimp sauce 57
  Chicken soup (delicate) 33
  Chicken soup (spicy) 124
  Chicken soup (very spicy) 34
  Chicken with spicy coconut milk gravy
    138
  Country captain 186
  Crisp-skin chicken 185
  Grilled chicken with hot spices 60
  Javanese-style fried chicken 56
  Piquant fried chicken 58

Roast spiced chicken 54
Satay-flavoured roast chicken 187
Spiced grilled chicken 55
Whole chicken curry 142
chickens, jointing 13
chillies 10, 206
  Beef in soy sauce and chillies 76
  bird's eye chillies 50, 206
  Chilli flower 23
  Chilli and peanut sauce 154
  chilli powder 206
  Chilli sauce 198
  Chilli-fried cauliflower 150
  Deep-fried prawns with chilli 183
  dried chillies 10, 34
  Eggs in chilli sauce 62
  Fish in brown bean sauce with stir-fried
    vegetables 36
  Fried chilli crabs 180
  Fried chilli sambal 112
  Grilled fish with chillies 42
  Hot chilli paste 104
  Pork and hot spices in coconut milk 195
  Prawns in chilli bean sauce 182
  Rojak 166, 199
  Squid fried with chillies 50
Chinese five-spice 207
Chinese sausages (lap cheong) 207
cilantro 207
cinnamon 207
cloves 207
coconut
  Bean sayur 93
  Chicken in coconut milk (Indonesian) 53
  Chicken in coconut milk (Malaysian) 140
  Chicken curry with toasted coconut 137
  Chicken with spicy coconut milk gravy
    138
  Coconut milk jelly 156
  Coconut milk soup 120
  Coconut rice 164
  Coconut sambal 149
  Coconut wafers 30
  Cooked vegetables with coconut 92
  Crisp spiced coconut with peanuts 111
  Crisp spiced coconut with peanuts (quick
    method) 111
  Dry-fried meat and coconut 70
  Fish in coconut milk and spices 41
  Fried fish with spicy coconut milk 46
  Fried prawns with coconut milk 48
  grated coconut 16, 162
  Meat and coconut patties 82
  Pineapple coconut curry 97
  Pork and hot spices in coconut milk 195
  Rice cooked in coconut milk with spices 20
  Rice rolls with spicy filling 25
  Satay-flavoured roast chicken 187
  Spiced coconut fish 130

Spicy cabbage in coconut milk 88
Vegetables in coconut sauce 87
Vegetables cooked in coconut milk with
  curry spices 96
coconut milk 8–9, 207
  making from scratch 9–10
coconut oil 7
Compressed rice cakes 121
Cooked vegetables with coconut 92
coriander (cilantro) 207
Corn fritters 28
Country captain 186
crab
  Fried chilli crabs 180
  Fried fish with crab sauce 178
Crisp skin chicken 185
Crisp spiced coconut with peanuts 111
  Quick method 111
croquettes, Eastern-style 189
Crunchy peanut sauce 107
cumin 207
curries
  Chicken and bamboo shoot curry 139
  Chicken curry with toasted coconut 137
  Dry-fried beef curry 72
  Dry-fried kidney curry 71
  Dry meat curry 74
  Fish curry 131
  Pineapple coconut curry 97
  Spicy mutton curry 146
  Squid curry 49
  Vegetable curry 148
  Vegetables cooked in coconut milk with
    curry spices 96
  Whole chicken curry 142
curry leaves 207

D

daging masak bali 66
daikon 207
daun salam 207
Deep-fried fish with vegetables 179
Deep-fried prawns with chilli 183
deep-frying 8
dendeng 77
dendeng ragi 70
desserts 117
  Agar-agar jelly 204
  Coconut milk jelly 156
  Many layered spice cake 114
  Sago pudding 158
  Silver fungus in sweet soup 204
  Toffee apples 202
Dried spiced meat 77
Dry-fried beef curry 72
Dry-fried kidney curry 71
Dry-fried meat and coconut 70
Dry meat curry 74

E

Eastern-style croquettes 189
egg noodles 12
  Noodle soup 167
eggplant
  Eggplant petjal 89
  Prawn and eggplant soup 32
eggs
  Egg roll wrappers 174
  Eggs in chilli sauce 62
  Eggs in soy sauce 63
  Many layered spice cake 114
  Marbled eggs 104
  Tofu omelettes 64
empal jawa 76

F

fennel 208
fenugreek 208
Festive yellow rice 23
fish
  Baked fish 43
  Balinese-style fish 38
  cutting fillets/steaks 13
  Deep-fried fish with vegetables 179
  dried fish (sprats) 207
  Fish in brown bean sauce with stir-fried
    vegetables 36
  fish cakes 208
  Fish in coconut milk and spices 41
  Fish curry 131
  Fish grilled in banana leaves 37
  Fish with peanut sauce 42
  fish sauce 208
  Fish in soy sauce 47
  Fried fish with crab sauce 178
  Fried fish with salted soy beans 128
  Fried fish sambal 132
  Fried fish with spicy coconut milk 46
  Grilled fish with chillies 42
  Grilled fish with spices 40
  Layered spiced fish and rice 127
  Spiced coconut fish 130
  Steamed fish (Straits Chinese style) 134
  Vinegared fish 134
  see also seafood
Fragrant rice 20
Fresh noodles, fried 165
Fresh rice noodle snack 165
Fresh spring rolls 174
Fried bananas 106
Fried chilli crabs 180
Fried chilli sambal 112
Fried fish with crab sauce 178
Fried fish with salted soy beans 128
Fried fish sambal 132
Fried fish with spicy coconut milk 46
Fried melinjo nut wafers 106

Fried noodles 22
Fried noodles, Singapore style 166
Fried onion flakes 105
Fried pork with rice vermicelli 190
Fried prawns with coconut milk 48
Fried rice 21
Fried rice noodles 122
Fried sweet potato balls 26
Fried tamarind pork (Bali) 78
Fried tofu with peanuts 98
Fried tofu with soy sauce 94
fruit salad, Spicy 108

G

gado-gado 95
galangal
  fresh 17
  greater 208
  lesser 208
garlic
  Crunchy peanut sauce 107
  frying 34
  grating 16
ghee (clarified butter) 208
ginger
  aromatic 208
  grating 16
glutinous rice 15, 208
Glutinous yellow rice 120
Green bean sambal 103
Grilled chicken with hot spices 60
Grilled fish with chillies 42
Grilled fish with spices 40
ground rice 210
gula melaka 158
gulai ayam 142
gulai ayam rebong 139
gulai cumi-cumi 49
gulai ikan 41, 131
gulai kambing 146
gulai manis kangkung 86

H

hoisin sauce 208
Hokkien mee soup 170
Hot chilli paste 104
Hot peanut sauce 110
Hot–sour prawn head sambal 102

I

ice kacang 116
ikan bali 38
ikan briani 127
ikan bumbu santan 46
ikan goreng taucheo 128
ikan kacang 42
ikan kecap 47
ikan kelapa 130
ikan kukus (Nonya) 134

ikan panggang (1) 37
ikan panggang (2) 40
ikan panggang pedis 42
Indonesia 14
  cuisine 14–16
ingredients 6
  Indonesian 17
  Malaysian 118
  Singaporean 160, 162

J

Javanese-style fried chicken 56
Javanese-style fried meatballs 80
jicama 211

K

kan bandeng 43
kari ayam kelapa 137
Kashmiri food 160
ketupat 121
kidneys: Dry-fried kidney curry 71
krupuk emping 106
krupuk udang 31

L

Lacy pancakes 153
laksa lemak 168
lamb satay, Madurese-style 82
laos powder 17, 208
lap cheong 207
lapis daging semarang 66
lard 7, 201
Layered spiced fish and rice 127
lemongrass 209
lemper 25
Lentil and mutton rissoles 143
liver: Spiced braised liver 138

M

mace 209
Madurese-style lamb satay 82
mah mee 167
Malay beef satay 144
Malaysian cuisine 116–17
mangosteens 15
Many layered spice cake 114
Marbled eggs 104
meat
  Dried spiced meat 77
  Dry-fried kidney curry 71
  Dry-fried meat and coconut 70
  Dry meat curry 74
  Fresh noodles, fried 165
  Fresh spring rolls 174
  Javanese-style fried meatballs 80
  Meat and coconut patties 82
  Noodle soup 167
  Rice rolls with spicy filling 25
  Shredded crisp-fried meat 68

Spiced braised liver 138
Spring rolls 171
Sweet satay 83
see also beef; lamb; mutton; pork
melinjo nuts 209
  Fried melinjo nut wafers 106
mie goreng 22
Mild peanut sauce 110
miso 209
Mixed seafood soup 168
murtaba 172
mushrooms, shiitake 209
mustard cabbage (chai goy) 209
mutton
  Mutton and lentil rissoles 143
  Spicy mutton curry 146

N

nasi goreng 21
nasi gurih 20
nasi kuning lengkap 23
nasi kunyit 120
nasi lemak 164
nasi putih 19
nasi uduk 20
Nonya cuisine 159–60, 161, 162
  Steamed fish (Straits Chinese style) 134
noodles 6, 12
  crisp-fried noodles 12
  dried cellophane (bean thread) noodles 12, 206
  dried egg noodles 12
  dried rice noodles 12
  dried rice vermicelli (rice-stick) noodles 12
  Fresh noodles, fried 165
  Fried noodles 22
  Fried noodles, Singapore style 166
  Hokkien mee soup 170
  Noodle soup 167
  soft-fried noodles 12
nutmeg 209

O

onion flakes, Fried 105
opor ayam 53
oyster sauce 209

P

pacari 97
palm sugar (jaggery) 117, 158, 209
  Coconut milk jelly 156
  Sago pudding 158
pancakes
  Lacy pancakes 153
  Sichuan pancakes 161
pandanus leaf 117, 164, 209
peanut oil 209
peanuts

Beef satay 191
Chilli and peanut sauce 154
Crisp spiced coconut with peanuts 111
Crisp spiced coconut with peanuts (quick method) 111
Crunchy peanut sauce 107
Fish with peanut sauce 42
Fried tofu with peanuts 98
Hot peanut sauce 110
Mild peanut sauce 110
Peanut wafers 30
Pork satay (Indonesian) 79
Pork satay (Singaporean) 191
Satay sauce 197
Vegetables with peanut sauce 95
pecal terung 89
pergedel goreng jawa 80
pergedel jagung 28
pickle, Vegetable 152
pilus 26
pindaing telur 63
Pineapple coconut curry 97
Piquant fried chicken 58
Piquant fried prawn sambal 103
pisang goreng 106
plum sauce 209
poh pia 174
pork
  Barbecue-style pork with black beans 194
  Fried pork with rice vermicelli 190
  Fried tamarind pork (Bali) 78
  Pork and hot spices in coconut milk 195
  Pork satay (Indonesian) 79
  Pork satay (Singaporean) 191
  Pork with Sichuan vegetables 188
  Spiced spareribs 192
prawns
  Chicken with shrimp sauce 57
  Deep-fried prawns with chilli 183
  Fried prawns with coconut milk 48
  Hokkien mee soup 170
  Hot–sour prawn head sambal 102
  Piquant fried prawn sambal 103
  Prawn crisps 31
  Prawn and eggplant soup 32
  Prawn fritters 27
  prawn powder 210
  Prawn and spinach soup 123
  Prawn stock 168
  Prawns in chilli bean sauce 182
  shrimp paste 210
  shrimp sauce 210
  Skewered grilled prawns 44
  Stir-fried prawns with bean sprouts and snow peas 176
  Sweet and sour fried prawns 177
pronunciation 7

R

rambutan 117
red Asian shallots 210
red food colouring powder 210
rempah 160
rempah-rempah 82
rempeyek 27
rempeyek kacang 30
rempeyek udang 27
rendang 74
rendang ayam 140
rendang daging 72
rendang ginjal 71
rice 6, 10–11
  Coconut rice 164
  Compressed rice cakes 121
  cooking methods 11, 15
  Festive yellow rice 23
  Fragrant rice 20
  Fried rice 21
  Glutinous yellow rice 120
  ground rice 210
  Layered spiced fish and rice 127
  old/new rice 10
  Rice cooked in coconut milk with spices
    20
  Rice rolls with spicy filling 25
  washing rice 11
  White rice 19
rice noodles 12
  Fresh rice noodle snack 165
  Fried rice noodles 122
  Singapore-style fried noodles 166
rice pullers 68
rice vermicelli (rice-stick) noodles 12, 210
  Fried pork with rice vermicelli 190
  Mixed seafood soup 168
  Pork with Sichuan vegetables 188
Roast spiced chicken 54
Rojak 166, 199
rosewater 210
roti flour 210
roti jala 153
Rotis with savoury filling 172
rujak buah-buah pedis 108

S

Sago pudding 158
sambal babi 195
sambal bajak 112, 210
sambal buncis 103
sambal cumi-cumi pedis 50
sambal goreng ikan 132
sambal goreng kembang 150
sambal goreng sotong 135
sambal goreng telur 62
sambal goreng udang 48
sambal goreng udang asam 103

sambal kelapa 149
sambal kepala udang 102
sambal ulek 104, 210
sambalan 101
sambals 15
  Basic sambal seasoning 101
  Chilli-fried cauliflower 150
  Coconut sambal 149
  Fried chilli sambal 112
  Fried fish sambal 132
  Green bean sambal 103
  Hot chilli paste (sambal ulek) 104
  Hot–sour prawn head sambal 102
  Piquant fried prawn sambal 103
  Pork and hot spices in coconut milk 195
  Squid sambal 135
satay daging 144
Satay-flavoured roast chicken 187
Satay sauce 197
saté ayam 61
saté babi 79
saté bumbu 84
saté kambing madura 82
saté manis 83
saté udang 44
sauces
  barbecue (char siu) sauce 206
  Chilli and peanut sauce 154
  Chilli sauce 198
  Crunchy peanut sauce 107
  hoisin sauce 208
  Hot peanut sauce 110
  Mild peanut sauce 110
  plum sauce 209
  Satay sauce 197
  shrimp sauce 210
  soy sauce 210–11
saus kacang (1) (Indonesian) 107
saus kacang (2) (Indonesian) 110
saus kacang (Malaysian) 154
saus kacang pedis 110
sayur buncis 93
sayur kari 96
sayur kol 88
sayur lodeh 87
sayur masak lemak 148
sayur tumis 90
sayur udang bayam 123
screwpine (pandanus) 117, 164, 209
seafood
  Fried chilli crabs 180
  Fried fish with crab sauce 178
  Mixed seafood soup 168
  Noodle soup 167
  Squid curry 49
  Squid fried with chillies 50
  Squid sambal 135
see also fish; prawns

Semarang-style sliced beef 66
semur ati 138
semur daging 73
serikaya dengan agar-agar 156
serundeng (1) 111
serundeng (2) 111
sesame oil 210
sesame seeds 210
shami kebab 143
shiitake mushrooms 209
Shredded crisp-fried meat 68
shrimp paste 210
shrimp sauce 210
  Chicken with shrimp sauce 57
Sichuan food 161
  Pork with Sichuan vegetables 188
silver fungus 210
  Silver fungus in sweet soup 204
Singapore 159–61
Singapore-style fried noodles 166
singgang ayam 55
singgang daging 67
skewers
  Beef satay 191
  Chicken grilled on skewers 61
  Madurese-style lamb satay 82
  Malay beef satay 144
  Pork satay 79, 191
  Skewered grilled prawns 44
  Spicy beef satay 84
  Sweet satay 83
sothi 120
soto ayam (1) (Indonesian) 33
soto ayam (2) (Indonesian) 34
soto ayam (Malaysian) 124
soup
  Chicken soup (delicate) 33
  Chicken soup (spicy) 124
  Chicken soup (very spicy) 34
  Coconut milk soup 120
  Hokkien mee soup 170
  Mixed seafood soup 168
  Noodle soup 167
  Prawn and eggplant soup 32
  Prawn and spinach soup 123
  Silver fungus in sweet soup 204
soy beans
  Beef cooked in soy sauce 73
  Beef in soy sauce and chillies 76
  Eggs in soy sauce 63
  Fish in brown bean sauce with stir-fried
    vegetables 36
  Fish in soy sauce 47
  Fried fish with salted soy beans 128
  Fried tofu with soy sauce 94
  salted soy beans (taucheo) 210
  soy sauce 210–11
  Tofu in salted soy bean paste 149

spekkoek kueh lapis 114
spice-grinding 16
Spiced braised liver 138
Spiced coconut fish 130
Spiced grilled chicken 55
Spiced spareribs 192
Spicy beef satay 84
Spicy cabbage in coconut milk 88
Spicy fruit salad 108
Spicy mutton curry 146
Spinach and prawn soup 123
sprats 207
spring roll pastry 211
Spring rolls 171
  Fresh 174
Squid curry 49
Squid fried with chillies 50
Squid sambal 135
star anise 211
star fruit 117
Steamed fish (Straits Chinese style) 134
Stir-fried prawns with bean sprouts and
    snow peas 176
Stir-fried vegetables 90
stock, Prawn 168
Straits Chinese style steamed fish 134
sugar cane juice 161
sweet potato balls, Fried 26
Sweet satay 83
Sweet and sour fried prawns 177
sweets, Indonesian 15

T

tahu goreng kacang 98
tahu goreng kecap 94
tahu telur 64
tamarind 211
  Basic sambal seasoning 101
  Dry-fried meat and coconut 70
  Fried chilli sambal 112
  Fried tamarind pork (Bali) 78
  Piquant fried prawn sambal 103
taucheo 210
  Fried fish with salted soy beans 128
  Tofu in salted soy bean paste 149
tauco ikan 36
taukwa dan taugeh 148
taukwa taucheo 149
telur berwarna 104
terung lodeh 32
Toffee apples 202
tofu 211
  Fresh spring rolls 174
  Fried tofu with peanuts 98
  Fried tofu with soy sauce 94
  Tofu and bean sprouts 148
  Tofu omelettes 64
  Tofu in salted soy bean paste 149
turmeric 211

U

urap 92
utensils
  Indonesian 16
  Malaysian 117
  Singaporean 161–2

V

vegetables
  Cooked vegetables with coconut 92
  Stir-fried vegetables 90
  Vegetable curry 148
  Vegetable pickle 152
  Vegetables in coconut sauce 87
  Vegetables cooked in coconut milk with
    curry spices 96
  Vegetables with peanut sauce 95
Vinegared fish 134

W

water chestnuts 211
Watercress in sweet gravy 86
White rice 19
Whole chicken curry 142
woks 7–8, 16, 162
  seasoning 7
wood ear fungus 211

Y

yam bean (jicama) 211